D1094133

PARADISE
LOST
IN OUR TIME

PARADISE LOST

IN OUR TIME

SOME COMMENTS

DOUGLAS BUSH

Gloucester, Mass.
PETER SMITH
1957

To the "sole Auditress"
who listened more than once

THE MESSENGER LECTURES

This book in its original form consisted of four lectures which the author delivered at Cornell University in the fall term of 1944, namely, the Messenger Lectures on the Evolution of Civilization. That series was founded and its title prescribed by Hiram J. Messenger, B.Litt., Ph.D., of Hartford, Connecticut, who directed in his will that a portion of his estate be given to Cornell University and used to provide annually "a course or courses of lectures on the evolution of civilization, for the special purpose of raising the moral standard of our political, business, and social life." The lectureship was established in 1923.

PREFACE

THESE discourses formed part of a much larger survey of Milton which was presented as one of the Lowell Institute's series in the autumn of 1943 and, with many changes, they were delivered as Messenger lectures at Cornell University in November, 1944. They are published in accordance with the terms of the Messenger lectureship. I must repeat in print my thanks to the administrators of both foundations for the honor of being invited, my appreciation of Cornell's cordial hospitality during a very pleasant visit, and my gratitude to the company of the elect and regenerate who made up staunch and sympathetic audiences.

It is doubtless unnecessary to say that four lectures offer only selective glimpses of *Paradise Lost* and of Milton. It is equally unnecessary, or at any rate impossible, to indicate my indebtedness to many scholars and critics.

For generous permission to quote from copyright books I am obliged to a number of publishers: to the Cambridge University Press and The Macmillan Company for quotations from Sir Herbert Grierson's *Milton and Wordsworth*; to Chatto and Windus for quotations from Dr. F. R. Leavis' *Revaluation* and Dr. E. M. W. Tillyard's *Poetry Direct and Oblique*; to Chatto and Windus and Harper and Brothers for the quotation from Mr. Aldous Huxley's *After Many a Summer Dies the Swan* (English title. *After Many a Summer*); to the Clarendon Press for quotations from Lord David Cecil's introduction to *The Oxford Book of Christian Verse* and Mr. T. S. Eliot's essay in *Essays and Studies by Members of the English Association*, volume XXI; to the Cresset Press and Robert M. McBride and Company for the quotation from Professor V. de Sola Pinto's *The English Renaissance, 1510–1688;* to Faber and Faber and Harcourt, Brace and Company for quotations from Mr. T. S. Eliot's *Collected Poems, Selected Essays, 1917–1932, Essays Ancient and Modern,* and *The Idea of a Christian Society;* to Harper and Brothers for the quotation from Sir Edward Marsh's *A Number of People;* to Houghton Mifflin Company for the quotation from C. E. Norton's translation of *The Divine Comedy;* to The Macmillan Company for quotations from Professor Whitehead's *Religion in the Making;* and to the Oxford University Press for quotations from Mr. J. Middleton Murry's *Studies in Keats New and Old* and Mr. C. S. Lewis' *A Preface to* Paradise Lost.

I must add a word of thanks to Cornell University Press for its editorial care and patient endurance of afterthoughts.

Douglas Bush

Cambridge, Massachusetts

CONTENTS

THE MODERN REACTION

AGAINST MILTON

AMONG THE GENERALITY OF PEOPLE the number who prefer *Paradise Lost* to the current best seller is probably smaller than the number who prefer Bach to a "name band," and no one would expect either group to be very large. But among the musical, even those who have an imperfect sympathy with Bach would not dream of sniffing at the *B Minor Mass*, while many of the literary sniff freely at *Paradise Lost*—though such persons, who shy away from Milton's biblical story and learned seriousness, will embrace with enthusiasm the often ponderous erudition and philosophizing of Thomas Mann's novel of Joseph. However, we are not much concerned with the legendary terrors which, in many minds, envelop a poet identified with religious themes and sublimity of imagination and tone. We are concerned with the critical reaction against Milton and *Paradise Lost* in particular which has been a very audible phenomenon of the past twenty-five years or more. That reaction, to be sure, has made small headway among those who really know Milton, and it has involved only a few critics, but it has for the most part been carried on with the kind of arrogant self-confidence which these same critics regard as one of Milton's central defects, and in literary criticism, as in other forms of propaganda, confident assertion goes a long way. So far as the reaction has embodied genuinely critical ideas, it has of course been salutary. We do not want to admire Milton or any other writer by tradition and blind faith, and if antagonism of any sort compels us to re-examine his credentials and our own feelings and opinions, it is all to the good.

This modern reaction is the subject of our first hour, and I must apologize to the audience, especially to those members of it who are here for the last time, for what seems the unavoidable necessity of approaching Milton by a controversial road. In the three lectures that follow, we shall be looking directly at Milton and much less at his critics, but it is impossible to discourse on *Paradise Lost* without taking account of the recent wave of hostility, a wave which appears to have carried a shoal of young intellectuals along with it. If there be any people who think that the rise or fall of Milton's fame is not of much moment in a war-torn world, we may remember that poetry has outlived many wars and that Milton is one of the great portions of that heritage for which the war has been fought, that, as Wordsworth wrote when Europe lay under the heel of Napoleon,

> We must be free or die, who speak the tongue
> That Shakespeare spake; the faith and morals hold
> Which Milton held.

Millions of people nowadays are anxious lest, having won the war, we fail to achieve lasting peace; but it would also be calamitous if, possessing such a poet and prophet as Milton, we should show ourselves unworthy of the possession. For indifference or hostility to him is not a mere matter of liking or disliking a particular poet; it belongs to the much larger question whether the tastes and standards of our generation reflect spiritual health or disease. It is rather doubtful if we do hold the faith and morals which Milton held.

Nineteenth-century liberalism often inclined critics of that age to recoil from Milton's religious beliefs, or supposed beliefs, while they celebrated his passion for liberty and his transcendent art and music. The modern critics have carried on one nineteenth-century impulse by summarily dismissing or denouncing Milton's religious ideas, and they have gone much further in attacking his poetic art as well. Their dethronement of Milton was necessary to the enthronement of Donne. The enormous modern vogue of Donne was in part solidly based on the great virtues of a kind of writing which had been inadequately appreciated. That kind of writing, to which the name "metaphysical" has long been attached, may be briefly defined as poetry which simultaneously embraces diverse planes of experience and is characterized by realistic immediacy, particularity, and complexity, by a fusion of thought and feeling, by the interplay of irony and wit, and by diction, syntax, and rhythms which belong to the genius of common speech. But the vogue of Donne, however solidly based, was attended with a good deal of extravagance, and with some degree of snob appeal;

many young people hastened to worship a difficult poet who had not been "clapper-clawed with the palms of the vulgar." That for Mr. T. S. Eliot the exaltation of one kind of writing should require the denigration of another is quite understandable, since a highly original poet can seldom enjoy poetry which is not akin to his own and which he cannot "use," but such narrowness of sensibility is rather less natural in Mr. Eliot's unpoetic satellites.

Donne was not the only representative of "metaphysical" poetry set up against the classicist Milton. There were Donne's successors and also, and especially, Dante, Shakespeare, and George Chapman. But the critics were not altogether consistent in their consideration of poetic art and poetic substance. They were sufficiently aware of the substance and meaning of poetry to be allergic to Milton's ideas as well as his style, but they did not apparently observe that their admired models of sensibility and expression, Dante, Shakespeare, and Chapman, were in their religious and ethical creed more or less close to Milton and very remote from most of themselves.

Further, the reaction against Milton coincided at some points with a reaction against the romantic poets of the early nineteenth century. To defeatist intellectuals of the "Armistice" period, 1918–1939, any form of idealism was anathema, whether romantic or Miltonic. The sceptical, cynical, and sensual irresponsibility of Jack Donne was, or seemed to be, very modern, and was much more congenial than either romantic faith in humanitarian progress or Milton's more strenuous and exacting faith in God, order, and individual righteousness.

While the personal opinions of a literary scholar, as he is frequently reminded by literary gentlemen, are of no account whatever, I should like, just to keep the record straight, to say that I have great admiration for Mr. Eliot's poetry and have more than once so testified in print; and that I have as much admiration for Donne as is good for anyone, and a perhaps excessive admiration for Chapman, Herbert, Vaughan, and Marvell. If I raise my voice against the sometimes fantastic adulation of Donne and the sometimes fantastic depreciation of Milton, it is not because I dislike metaphysical poetry. I have merely pointed out some of the less valid reasons which have gone along with valid ones in establishing the cult of Donne; and I do not think that a right view of Milton's greatness necessitates uncritical disparagement of the metaphysicals, or vice versa. I do think that the house of poetry, non-dramatic poetry, has many mansions, and that Milton still occupies the royal suite. And I think it is important for us in these times that we should relive the experience of Milton, that a multitude of readers to whom he can give much should not be alienated by a small but dogmatic chorus of opinion. There is indeed ground for belief that the righting of our poetical perspective was under way before the war began, and that the war will be found to have completed the process. Viewed against the scope and stress of a world conflict, Milton's stature, and Donne's, somehow assume their true proportions.

Whether or not that belief commands assent, we are considering the modern reaction against Milton. With that movement one would certainly not associate Mr. Oliver Elton and Sir Herbert Grierson, yet these eminent scholar-critics may be mentioned as men of nineteenth-century vintage who, with all their aesthetic admiration, have apparently been unable to see in *Paradise Lost* a great religious poem. And the late Archbishop of Canterbury doubtless spoke for some laymen when he declared that Milton's longer poems bored him stiff. But the active campaign against Milton has been conducted by younger guerrilla warriors. We might begin by naming Mr. Ezra Pound, though we shall pass him by, since his notion of Milton is not of much more value than his notion of, say, his own learning or of Fascism. Nor shall we linger with Mr. Herbert Read, whose studies of Wordsworth and Shelley indicate some capacity for aberration, and whose opinion of Milton is comprehended in that of critics to be mentioned later. Mr. Wilson Knight is a fire worshiper whom *Paradise Lost* leaves cold, or at least with a mixture of chills and fever. In 1939 Mr. Knight produced a long critique, mainly of the epic, entitled "The Frozen Labyrinth." In 1942, having felt the impact of the war, Mr. Knight mounted the architect of the frozen labyrinth in a chariot of wrath as the great apostle of national liberty and destiny. One may respect the feeling behind the change while thinking that Milton might have preferred relatively intelligible criticism to a whirlwind apotheosis.

For a clear statement of a common attitude we may go to Mr. Middleton Murry. Mr. Murry acknowledges some sort of greatness in Milton, but sees in him a repellent type of secularized Protestantism:

6

. . . his apparent peculiarity is that he is overweeningly confident in the natural man, or at least in the natural reason of man. . . .

On the moral and spiritual side I find it easy enough to place him: he is, simply, a bad man of a very particular kind, who is a bad man because he is so sublimely certain of being a good one. . . . But these defences of Milton teach us nothing; they tell us nothing new. They are irrelevant to our dissatisfaction with Milton: which is that a poet so evidently great, in some valid sense of the word, should have so little intimate meaning for us. We cannot make him real. He does not, either in his great effects or his little ones, touch our depths. He demonstrates, but he never reveals. He describes beauty beautifully; but truth never becomes beauty at his touch.[1]

This judgment is typical of both the religious romantic and the secular romantic. Mr. F. R. Leavis expresses a similar dislike of Milton:

He has 'character,' moral grandeur, moral force; but he is, for the purposes of his undertaking, disastrously single-minded and simple-minded. He reveals everywhere a dominating sense of righteousness and a complete incapacity to question or explore its significance and conditions. This defect of intelligence is a defect of imagination. He offers as ultimate for our worship mere brute assertive will, though he condemns it unwittingly by his argument and by glimpses of his own finer human standard. His volume of moral passion owes its strength too much to innocence—a guileless un-

---

[1] *Studies in Keats New and Old* (2d ed.; London: Oxford University Press, 1939), pp. 110, 121–122. First published in 1930.

7

awareness of the subtleties of egotism—to be an apt agent for projecting an 'ordered whole of experience.' [2]

But Mr. Leavis is more interested in the technique and tone of poetry than in its moral values, and his main concern is the stiff, heavy English of *Paradise Lost*.

A further roll call of rebel angels would indicate that they say pretty much the same things, and we shall give our attention to two or three representatives. Much the most important, both in priority and in authority, is Mr. Eliot. Mr. Leavis' essay, cited a moment ago, begins with these smug words:

Milton's dislodgment, in the past decade, after his two centuries of predominance, was effected with remarkably little fuss. The irresistible argument was, of course, Mr. Eliot's creative achievement; it gave his few critical asides—potent, it is true, by context—their finality, and made it unnecessary to elaborate a case.

Apparently Mr. Eliot's critical asides, though potent, were not quite final, since the complete demolition of Milton required twenty-five pages from Mr. Leavis. However, the central fact was that the poetic world was not big enough to contain both Milton and Mr. Eliot, and Milton had to go. Whatever the motives of Mr. Eliot's camp followers and others, his own sniping at Milton has been a kind of oblique—and quite needless—justification of his own poetry.

Perhaps the most potent of all Mr. Eliot's ideas was

---

[2] *Revaluation: Tradition & Development in English Poetry* (London: Chatto and Windus, 1936), p. 58. The essay first appeared in *Scrutiny* in 1933.

that, in the unified sensibility of the metaphysical poets, thought and feeling and the most diverse kinds of experience were fused, whereas Milton, who lacked that capacious and flexible sensibility, made a baneful divorce between thought and feeling and imposed that dissociation upon his successors up to our own day. Such a doctrine, involving not only the metaphysicals and Milton but the whole range of English poets, would seem to require a considerable analysis of a vast and various body of writing before it could be launched even as a hypothesis. But Mr. Eliot covered the ground in a few pages or paragraphs, and among all moderns who profess critical intelligence this has been a standard dogma ever since. One might exclaim, as Dr. Johnson did about Goldsmith's debts, "Was ever poet so trusted before?" Of Mr. Eliot's place in poetry there can be no question, and his criticism is already classical in one sense; it has become a part of English literary history because it has been the main agent in effecting a revolution in taste. But the other or "classicist" meaning of "classical" seems rather less evident. Although Mr. Eliot has chosen that label for himself and wears the mantle of authority, his critical essays, with all their ordered lucidity and insight and impersonal traditionalism, are not seldom more valuable in illuminating their author than in illuminating their subjects. They may be utterances of that "Inner Voice" for which Mr. Eliot once chided Mr. Murry and others, and to the inner voice one may, in Mr. Eliot's own phrase, remain an inner deaf-mute.

In 1936 Mr. Eliot went about the business of iconoclasm more directly in a short essay called "A Note on the

Verse of John Milton." [3] The modest title is a reminder
that a commando raid by Mr. Eliot is equivalent to full-
scale invasion. While Milton is not, apparently, a good
poet, he is admitted, reluctantly, to be a very great one,
but, like Mr. Murry, Mr. Eliot is puzzled to decide
in what Milton's greatness consists:

As a man, he is antipathetic. Either from the moralist's point
of view, or from the theologian's point of view, or from the
psychologist's point of view, or from that of the political
philosopher, or judging by the ordinary standards of likeable-
ness in human beings, Milton is unsatisfactory.

If we are not disposed to accept a simple "Off with his
head!" we may ask to what kind of moralist, theologian,
psychologist, political philosopher, and human being
Milton is unsatisfactory. All that emerges from the supposedly universal verdict is that Mr. Eliot does not like
the mind and personality of Milton; and his way of saying
so illustrates his agreement with the remark he once
quoted from Remy de Gourmont, that it is a man's great
effort, if he is sincere, to erect his personal impressions
into laws.

As theologian and political thinker Milton may be
antipathetic to Mr. Eliot, as he was on similar grounds to
Dr. Johnson; it does not follow that he is antipathetic to
a large number of other intelligent people. As for "the
psychologist," all of us rest under his disapproval, and the
nature of Milton's special obliquity one may be unable to
guess. What indictment can be lodged by "the moralist"

---

[3] *Essays and Studies by Members of the English Association,*
XXI (Oxford: Clarendon Press, 1936).

is not clear, unless it is that, like some of the Church fathers, Milton could be violent in controversy and that, like some other upright men, he accepted the execution of King Charles.[4] If these things are what disturbed Mr. Eliot's "moralist," we may observe that, in writing a eulogy of Lancelot Andrewes and his sermons, Mr. Eliot did not think it necessary to mention what has troubled other admirers, the saintly bishop's approval of the infamous Countess of Essex' infamous plea for divorce and his acceptance of, or share in, the sending of a heretic to the stake.

Finally, although Mr. Eliot may not like what he knows of Milton as a human being (and although one may doubt if Isaiah or Aeschylus or Dante was very likeable), there is plentiful evidence in Milton's writings and in the early biographies that he liked and was liked by a varied circle of friends, that he had, as Miss Darbishire says, the genius

---

[4] It may be added that Milton's character and career have been scanned with peculiar zeal by a Swedish and a French scholar, and that the main charges they have been able to manufacture are: first, that Milton could not have visited Galileo as he said he had because the scientist was kept under surveillance—a kind of circumstantial argument which, applied to a case three centuries old, seems rather nebulous; and, secondly, that Milton, with the President of the Council, contrived to have a prayer from Sidney's *Arcadia* inserted in some issues of *Eikon Basilike* in order that Milton could "smear" that dangerous book by exposing the passage. Without going into this matter, one can say that the witness invoked was a notorious rogue and that the modern arguments, apart from any question of Milton's character, do not even make sense in themselves. A recent and vigorous discussion of the case is R. W. Chambers, "Poets and their Critics: Langland and Milton," *Proceedings of the British Academy*, XXVII (1941).

for friendship. And his funeral was attended not only by "all his learned and great friends" but by "a friendly concourse of the vulgar." [5]

So much for Milton the bad man. Since it is axiomatic in modern criticism that our concern is with an author's works and not his personal character, this would seem an irrelevant topic if it were not that the anti-Miltonists use their prejudice against the man as a ready and easy way to establish a prejudice against his poetry. They seldom use that approach to Donne, in spite of the abundant material at hand—and quite apart from Donne's early libertinism, which is indeed an asset, being so much more human and attractive than Milton's strict virtue. I have no desire to prove Milton a saint, which he was not. But those of us who do not feel qualified to cast stones at him might pause for a minute to recall another judgment, familiar though it is, delivered by a man nearer to Milton in literary stature, as well as in time, than any modern:

> Milton! thou shouldst be living at this hour:
> England hath need of thee: she is a fen
> Of stagnant waters: altar, sword, and pen,
> Fireside, the heroic wealth of hall and bower,
> Have forfeited their ancient English dower

---

[5] A little later Mr. Eliot speaks of "the peculiar education" Milton received as one of his liabilities. It was the same kind of education as that of the other seventeenth-century poets whom Mr. Eliot admires, the kind of classical-Christian education which Mr. Eliot has written two admirable essays to uphold as a prime need of our time. There was nothing in the least peculiar about Milton's education, unless that it was broader, and pursued with more intensity, than some other men's.

Of inward happiness. We are selfish men;
Oh! raise us up, return to us again;
And give us manners, virtue, freedom, power.
Thy soul was like a Star, and dwelt apart;
Thou hadst a voice whose sound was like the sea:
Pure as the naked heavens, majestic, free,
So didst thou travel on life's common way,
In cheerful godliness; and yet thy heart
The lowliest duties on herself did lay.

We may ask ourselves which view of Milton comes nearer the mark.

Having disposed of Milton the man and the thinker, Mr. Eliot speaks of his bad influence. As regards the pseudo-Miltonism of many eighteenth-century poets, he admits that a good deal of the responsibility may devolve upon those poets themselves, but he affirms that "Milton's poetry could *only* be an influence for the worse, upon any poet whatever . . . that Milton's bad influence may be traced much farther than the eighteenth century, and much farther than upon bad poets," and that it is "an influence against which we still have to struggle." Mr. Eliot seems to have forgotten his own dictum, uttered apropos of Seneca, that "the influence of any man is a different thing from himself"; [6] and we should hesitate to blame Mr. Eliot for the not always successful efforts of his imitators.

But all our guns are spiked by the next pronouncement. Of what the critic has to say against Milton he considers

---

[6] *Selected Essays, 1917–1932* (London: Faber and Faber, 1932), pp. 132–133; (New York: Harcourt, Brace, 1932), p. 113. In later remarks on Milton (see page 23 below), Mr. Eliot takes his earlier and sounder position.

that "the only jury of judgement is that of the ablest poetical practitioners" of his own time! One defect in the logic of this declaration has been pointed out by Mr. C. S. Lewis—that we cannot, on such terms, even know who are the ablest poetical practitioners of our time, or whether Mr. Eliot is a poet, nor can Mr. Eliot himself know without begging the question. Another large fallacy is less abstract. Throughout the eighteenth and nineteenth and early twentieth centuries a successive series of Eliots might have appealed to the judgment of the ablest poetical practitioners of their times, and they would have got a series of unanimous or almost unanimous verdicts that Milton was the greatest and best of English nondramatic poets. It appears, however, that almost the whole array of English poets for over two hundred years were merely wrong, while the judgment of the ablest poets of our time is infallible and final. Who make up this great tribunal Mr. Eliot does not indicate. The only modern poet mentioned in the essay is Mr. Pound, whose infallibility we may be forgiven for doubting. If other able poets of our time have testified against Milton, I do not remember their names; but I do remember that such modernist poets as Allen Tate, John Crowe Ransom, and Yvor Winters have manifested their admiration. Again, under the show of authority, we are listening to Mr. Eliot's inner voice.

The main thesis of Mr. Eliot's essay is that throughout his poetry Milton lacks a visual imagination and that he sacrifices to sound the naturalness of speech and the vitality of words; whereas Shakespeare conveys the feeling of being in a particular place at a particular time, and offers perpetual novelty in his combinations of words, Milton's language is vague, artificial, and conventional. One hardly needs to point out how uncritical is the anti-Miltonist habit here illustrated, the open or tacit setting up of Shakespeare's realistic dramatic speech as a standard by which to try the wholly different nondramatic poetry of Milton—though one might expect the author of *The Waste Land* and *Ash-Wednesday*, *Murder in the Cathedral* and *The Family Reunion*, to be aware of such a fundamental difference.

Mr. Eliot first quotes the lines from *Macbeth* on "The temple-haunting martlet" and "Light thickens," and then, by way of contrast with Shakespeare's naturalness and particularity, gives us three bits of conventional artifice from Milton's early work. One is a line from a lyric in the little masque, *Arcades*—

O'er the smooth enamell'd green—

in which "enamell'd" is marked for censure. Since Marvell has all the virtues Milton lacks, and has none of the Miltonic vices, we may wonder if Mr. Eliot also condemns Marvell's picture of Bermuda:

He gave us this eternal Spring,
Which here enamels every thing.

Milton is not trying to make us see and feel grass; he wishes, like Marvell, to suggest something finer than mere nature provides.

Mr. Eliot's second example of conventional artifice is from the opening of *Comus:*

                    paths of this drear Wood,
    The nodding horror of whose shady brows
    Threats the forlorn and wand'ring Passenger.

Milton is personifying his symbolic wood by way of
heightening its sinister darkness. Mr. Eliot presumably
does not like "nodding horror," presumably because he
sees the phrase as a bit of eighteenth-century poetic diction. But at the time Milton was writing it was a novelty.
As Mr. Geoffrey Tillotson has shown, the use of English
derivatives in their classical meaning was beginning in the
early seventeenth century, and such words—like some of
Mr. Eliot's classicisms of diction—had an effect compa-
rable to the metaphysical wit and surprise. Granted that
these lines of Milton's have no special distinction, they
show already a touch of that suggestive vagueness which
can be as essential for its purpose as particularity.

That Mr. Eliot's demand for particularity is purely
arbitrary dogma is made very clear by his third example.
The imagery in "L'Allegro" and "Il Penseroso," he says,
is all general, and he quotes:

            While the Plowman near at hand,
            Whistles o'er the Furrow'd Land,
            And the Milkmaid singeth blithe,
            And the Mower whets his scythe,
            And every Shepherd tells his tale
            Under the Hawthorn in the dale.

Mr. Eliot must surely be the only critic who ever com-
plained of these buoyant lines. "It is not," he says, "a
particular ploughman, milkmaid, and shepherd that

Milton sees (as Wordsworth might see them); the sensuous effect of these verses is entirely on the ear, and is joined to the concepts of ploughman, milkmaid, and shepherd." One would have thought it obvious that realistic particularity would be quite out of place in a "landscape with figures," in ideal pictures designed to express and evoke contrasted moods. One wonders if the ploughman should have been individualized with the swollen ankles of Simon Lee, or if the name of poetry should be denied to such generalized pastoral images as: "The Lord is my shepherd; I shall not want. He maketh me to lie down in green pastures: he leadeth me beside the still waters."

The lack of new life in Milton's language, Mr. Eliot continues, appears even in his most mature work, and he quotes *Samson Agonistes:*

> The Sun to me is dark
> And silent as the Moon,
> When she deserts the night,
> Hid in her vacant interlunar cave.

The description of the moon's darkness as silence, an arresting figure used by Virgil and Dante, gains fresh power, as Mr. Tillyard points out, on the lips of the blind Samson. But what Mr. Eliot dislikes is "vacant" and "cave," and his dislike—to follow Mr. Tillyard further—arises from ignorance of the ancient astronomical idea Milton employs, that of the moon's retiring into a cave between her bright appearances, an idea which is here related, with concentrated, subtle, and ironic indirectness, to Samson's present but temporary impotence.[7]

A tortuous style, says Mr. Eliot, is not necessarily a dead one, when its peculiarity is aimed at precision; only when complication is dictated by a demand of verbal music, instead of by any demand of sense. He then compares a speech of Satan's with a passage in Henry James, whose intricate utterance is aimed at precision and not merely at sound. The complication of a Miltonic sentence, on the other hand, is "a complication deliberately introduced into what was a previously simplified and abstract thought. The dark angel here is not *thinking* or conversing, but making a speech carefully prepared for him; and the arrangement is for the sake of musical value, not for significance. A straightforward utterance, as of a Homeric or Dantesque character, would make the speaker very much more real to us; but reality is no part of the intention." This is the Miltonic speech, a speech delivered by Satan to his followers after God has proclaimed Christ as His Son and the Messiah:

> Thrones, Dominations, Princedoms, Virtues, Powers,
> If these magnific Titles yet remain
> Not merely titular, since by Decree
> Another now hath to himself ingross't
> All Power, and us eclipst under the name
> Of King anointed, for whom all this haste
> Of midnight march, and hurried meeting here,
> This only to consult how we may best

---

[7] E. M. W. Tillyard, *The Miltonic Setting Past and Present* (Cambridge University Press; New York: Macmillan, 1938), pp. 101–102.

> With what may be devis'd of honours new
> Receive him coming to receive from us
> Knee-tribute yet unpaid, prostration vile,
> Too much to one, but double how endur'd,
> To one and to his image now proclaim'd?

One may be unable to see what is complicated or tortuous in these lines. The sense is plain and the whole speech reveals Satan's thwarted ambition and passionate resentment. Further, the critic has failed to grasp Milton's intention. We are told that Satan is not thinking or conversing, as he should be. Of course he is not. He is the leader of a rebellion making a speech of exhortation to his followers, flattering and arousing them by recalling what splendid titles and powers they have enjoyed and are now being deprived of. In such a situation rhetorical magniloquence is essential to the effect he desires. We might, by the way, put beside Milton part of "a straightforward utterance" from Dante:

The next triad, that in like manner bourgeons in this sempiternal spring which the nightly Aries despoils not, perpetually sing Hosannah with three melodies, which sound in the three orders of joy wherewith it is threefold. In this hierarchy are the three divinities, first Dominations, and then Virtues; the third order is of Powers. Then, in the two penultimate dances, the Principalities and Archangels circle; the last is wholly of Angelic sports. These orders all gaze upward, and downward so prevail, that toward God all are drawn, and all draw.[8]

---

[8] *The Divine Comedy*, tr. C. E. Norton (Boston: Houghton Mifflin, 1902), *Paradise*, xxviii.

Is this speaker so obviously "thinking or conversing," even in the lucidity of a prose translation? Is she so "very much more real to us" than the angry Satan?

Mr. Eliot quotes two more specimens of Milton's rhetoric. One is the geographical passage in the eleventh book of *Paradise Lost* where Michael, beginning his revelation of human history to Adam, takes him up a high hill like that

> Whereon for different cause the Tempter set
> Our second Adam in the Wilderness,
> To show him all Earth's Kingdoms and thir Glory.

We could not have a plainer declaration of Milton's purpose. Then comes the compendious and suggestive survey of the great empires and rich cities of the world, the realms of khan and mogul, czar and sultan, all symbols of the power and pomp and vanity of earthly kings and all familiar in history and books of travel. And this is what Mr. Eliot (with the support of that sensitive Miltonic critic, Richard Bentley) pronounces not serious poetry, but rather a solemn game.[9]

The other passage is from "Lycidas":

> Whether beyond the stormy Hebrides,
> Where thou perhaps under the whelming tide
> Visit'st the bottom of the monstrous world;
> Or whether thou to our moist vows denied,
> Sleep'st by the fable of Bellerus old,
> Where the great vision of the guarded Mount
> Looks toward Namancos and Bayona's hold.

---

[9] Cf. Tillyard, *The Miltonic Setting*, p. 93.

"Than which," says Mr. Eliot, "for the single effect of grandeur of sound, there is nothing finer in poetry." The critic's thesis makes this left-handed praise. He does not observe that the geographical allusions are presented with great visual power, the full power of the best Miltonic mixture of the precise and the vague. Nor does he perceive that the purpose and effect of these allusions, which are only—and greatly—heightened by the sound, are to give us an overwhelming sense of the littleness and helplessness of man in a world of natural forces which God does not seem to control. Finally, we might ask if these lines are an example of Milton's pervasive deadness of language, or of his pervasive failure to fuse thought and feeling?

Mr. Eliot's general conclusions must be quoted in full:

A disadvantage of the rhetorical style appears to be, that a dislocation takes place, through the hypertrophy of the auditory imagination at the expense of the visual and tactile, so that the inner meaning is separated from the surface, and tends to become something occult, or at least without effect upon the reader until fully understood. To extract everything possible from *Paradise Lost*, it would seem necessary to read it in two different ways, first solely for the sound, and second for the sense. The full beauty of his long periods can hardly be enjoyed while we are wrestling with the meaning as well; and for the pleasure of the ear the meaning is hardly necessary, except in so far as certain key-words indicate the emotional tone of the passage. Now Shakespeare, or Dante, will bear innumerable readings, but at each reading all the elements of appreciation can be present. There is no interruption between the surface that these poets present to you and the core. While, therefore, I cannot pretend to have

penetrated to any 'secret' of these poets, I feel that such appreciation of their work as I am capable of points in the right
direction; whereas I cannot feel that my appreciation of
Milton leads anywhere outside of the mazes of sound. That,
I feel, would be the matter for a separate study, like that of
Blake's prophetic books; it might be well worth the trouble,
but would have little to do with my interest in the poetry.
So far as I perceive anything, it is a glimpse of a theology
that I find in large part repellent, expressed through a mythology which would have been better left in the Book of Genesis, upon which Milton has not improved. There seems to
me to be a division, in Milton, between the philosopher or
theologian and the poet . . .

This curious mixture of ultrasophistication and naïveté
leaves us with the exponent of an odious theology who has
only one gift, that of creating mazes of sound. It is a verdict
we might have expected Mr. Eliot to render upon Swin-
burne. It is puzzling to guess how he could call Milton a
very great poet indeed.

To go through an essay item by item, in the fashion of
a seventeenth-century controversialist, is not a correct or
mature or exciting procedure, but it has this advantage: it
enables us to say that every time Mr. Eliot quotes and directly comments upon the text of Milton he clearly betrays
a lack of perception and understanding. And these misread
bits of Milton are the representative basis of his large
generalizations. When all his evidence is unreliable, not
even a jury of poets could give authority to his judgment.
Would Mr. Eliot accept the judgments of a critic who
read his own poetry, or that of his favorites, in the same
spirit?

It should be said here that in his wise address to the Classical Association in 1942 Mr. Eliot coupled Shakespeare and Milton as our two greatest poets, and in a paragraph on Milton uttered what may have amounted to a palinode.[10] But even such a palinode, if it was one, cannot alter the fact that Mr. Eliot has done more than any other individual to turn a generation away from Milton—a fact doubly regrettable because Mr. Eliot and Milton, as poets in the classical-Christian tradition, are indissolubly allied against naturalistic disorder.

The unsupported, unexamined generalizations that we have reviewed are the kind of thing which passes current among anti-Miltonists, who follow the well-known principle that what they tell us three times must be true. Let us take one further example, which might be called semi-official, since it comes from the introduction to the *Oxford Book of Christian Verse* (1940). In surveying his chief writers the editor, Lord David Cecil, says:

Donne takes first place among English Christian poets. For he alone is equally interesting as Christian and as poet. . . . And religion was to him so stimulating a subject that there was hardly an aspect of it that did not fire him to poetry.

We shall not pause to question these very questionable remarks but will proceed to what is of more direct interest. Milton, Lord David declares,

was not essentially a religious poet. He was a philosopher rather than a devotee. His imagination was lucid and con-

---

[10] *The Classics and the Man of Letters* (London: Oxford University Press, 1942).

crete, unlit by heavenly gleams; theology to him was a superior branch of political science, the rule of reason and the moral law as exhibited in the working of the cosmos. Nor was his moral sensibility a Christian one. The Stoic virtues, fortitude, temperance, above all, moral independence, were what he valued. He did not live by faith, scorned hope, and was indisposed to charity; while pride, so far from being the vice which Christianity considers it, was to Milton the mark of a superior nature. As an exponent of the Christian spirit he cannot compare with Donne or Herbert. But if he is not our greatest religious poet, he is the greatest of English poets who have made religion their subject. . . . As an exposition of Christian belief *Paradise Lost* and *Paradise Regained* are failures. In *Paradise Lost* All-holy God and innocent Adam are made equally irritable and egotistic; Christ in *Paradise Regained* is an austere, unsympathetic classical philosopher. But for mastery of design, for distinction of style, for sustained grandeur of conception, Milton surpasses every other poet whose works are quoted in this collection.[11]

Here we have the good old story, considerably heightened on the adverse side. Not to speak of other matters of opinion or prejudice, on which one could say something, one would like some evidence for the assertion concerning Milton's want of faith, hope, and even charity (the anti-Miltonists' own peculiar virtue!) and his high esteem for unchristian pride. The nature of the poet's religious thought and feeling had been made pretty clear, before Lord David wrote, by a number of Miltonists, but one surmises that his pronouncements were based on boy-

---

[11] *Oxford Book of Christian Verse* (Oxford: Clarendon Press, 1940), pp. xvii, xxi–xxii.

hood recollections of Milton and Sir Walter Raleigh's book. The anti-Miltonists in general, like Congreve's Petulant, do not need learning, they rely altogether on their parts. It is worth noting that the author of a leading article on Lord David's book, in the semiofficial organ of English criticism, the London *Times Literary Supplement*, quoted some of his chief dicta on Milton and acquiesced in them as a matter of course, with only a slight peripheral qualification. So long as such ex-cathedra verdicts can be delivered from such quarters, so long are mere scholars justified in opposing them.

Since this hostility to Milton has developed almost wholly in his own country,[12] and since such Englishmen as Messrs. Tillyard, Charles Williams, C. S. Lewis, and R. W. Chambers—not to mention the work of American scholars—have written sensitive and cogent expositions and defenses of Milton, it may be said, or thought, that there can be no occasion for another and inevitably less sensitive and cogent defense. There is no adequate reply to that. But by way of extenuation one may say, first, that one has one's own view of Milton and feels moved to express it; secondly, that most "general readers" here as well as in England seem to rest in the nineteenth-century notion of verbal and musical beauties divorced from obsolete substance; and, thirdly, that a good many bright American undergraduates have been infected by the modernist reaction and of late years have poured forth with monotonous glibness the dogmas of the "metaphys-

---

[12] One might add such a piece of crude fictional slander as Robert Graves's *Wife to Mr. Milton* (London: Cassell, 1943; New York: Creative Age Press, 1944).

ical" and anti-Miltonist creed—though it should be added that some other bright, or perhaps brighter, undergraduates have remained proof against the fear of holding an unfashionable opinion.

Much as I should like to speak of Milton's other works, early and late, we are focusing our attention upon *Paradise Lost* because it has borne the brunt of the attack. And we shall look first at some of the central principles of Milton's religious and ethical thought. If any excuse be needed for such a natural enterprise, we may find one in the opening words of Mr. Eliot's essay on "Religion and Literature":

Literary criticism should be completed by criticism from a definite ethical and theological standpoint. In so far as in any age there is common agreement on ethical and theological matters, so far can literary criticism be substantive. In ages like our own, in which there is no such common agreement, it is the more necessary for Christian readers to scrutinize their reading, especially of works of imagination, with explicit ethical and theological standards. The "greatness" of literature cannot be determined solely by literary standards; though we must remember that whether it is literature or not can be determined only by literary standards.[18]

As we have seen, Mr. Eliot allows that Milton belongs, in a pernicious way, to literature, but he contradicts the sound theory just quoted by saying that the exploration of Milton's repellent ideas would have little to do with his own interest in the poetry. In the face of such inconsist-

---

[18] *Essays Ancient and Modern* (London: Faber and Faber, 1936), p. 93; (New York: Harcourt, Brace, 1936), p. 92.

ency we can only appeal from Philip prejudiced to Philip unprejudiced.

If we needed any negative excuse for considering Milton's thought, in addition to that provided by the anti-Miltonists' unanimous ignorance, we might find it in Mr. Logan Pearsall Smith's *Milton and His Modern Critics* (1940–1941). On the positive side of his argument Mr. Smith did not go much beyond an ardent but rather slight eulogy of Milton's art and music. Milton was assuredly always an artist, and in general, most of us may think, a great artist, but he did not prayerfully and repeatedly dedicate his life and faculties to the manipulation of vowels and consonants. If a reputedly great poet has no other claim upon us than his style and sound, however wonderful these may be, we might better admit that he is dead and read poets who still have something to say. But before we assent too readily to the conventional view that *Paradise Lost* is a monument to dead ideas, and the poet's art the decoration on a tomb, we may ask, first, what those ideas were, and, secondly, if they are in essence so remote from us and our world, if they are not, rather, very close to what many modern thinkers have been declaring are necessary to our own necessary regeneration. Nowadays old and young are full of zeal for a better world, and that of course is fine. But, to judge from the millions of words poured into print and into the air, much of that zeal is directed toward making other people better, or making more and better gadgets. In all his major poems Milton is occupied with the far more real and fundamental problem of making one's self better. And he makes us better not merely through his imaginative and "poetical" beauties but through the total effect of his religious and ethical theme, through his profound concern with "man, the heart of man, and human life."

II

RELIGIOUS AND ETHICAL

PRINCIPLES

SINCE *Paradise Lost* is so commonly regarded as a pictorial tapestry or musical score with an unfortunate
basis of dead and repellent ideas, I said that we would look
at those ideas. In attempting to describe, not the complex
body of Milton's thought, but a few central principles, I
do not mean to imply that *Paradise Lost* should be read as
a theological or philosophic treatise; nor do I mean that, as
a poem, it can now be read in the same spirit in which it was
composed—one would not make that claim for the works
of Homer or Virgil or Dante or Shakespeare. But I do
mean that the quality of Milton's poetry is inseparable
from his vision of life, and that his vision of life, in its
essentials, remains significant, whatever the changes in our
ways of thought—and indeed to a large measure because
these have changed so much. *Paradise Lost* may be a
dilapidated museum with a few fine exhibits scattered
along the mouldy shelves, or it may be a temple of religious
thought and feeling of which the modern reader has lost
the key. At the present time we have a multitude of serious
minor poets, who mirror the supposedly overwhelming

complexities of the modern world, but we do not hear any voice of heroic magnitude proclaiming that good is good and evil evil, that man is a religious and moral being in a religious and moral universe, and that the destiny of the race depends upon the individual soul. To be moved by the poetic presentation of such elementary convictions is to enjoy the experience which all great poetry gives, and it is also, perhaps, to be rid of some factitious complexities.

There is small need to emphasize Milton's conception of the high office of the poet-priest. No other poet of the Renaissance held that traditional conception with such exalted religious fervor. To recall one of his many passages on the subject, in 1641–1642, when he realized that he must defer the great poem of which he had dreamed, he set it apart not only from the amorous and complimentary verse of contemporary cavaliers but from the epics of the great pagans who had lacked the illumination of Christian faith. What he planned was

a work not to be raised from the heat of youth, or the vapors of wine; like that which flows at waste from the pen of some vulgar amorist, or the trencher fury of a rhyming parasite; nor to be obtained by the invocation of dame memory and her siren daughters, but by devout prayer to that eternal Spirit, who can enrich with all utterance and knowledge, and sends out his seraphim, with the hallowed fire of his altar, to touch and purify the lips of whom he pleases.

That is the kind of poet we are dealing with. The critics who are always talking of Milton's pride and egotism—though they never furnish evidence—would doubtless regard this as a good specimen. It is, on the contrary, an eloquent example of his deeply religious humility.

It may be admitted at the start that the main principles of Milton's religious philosophy, while familiar to students of Renaissance thought, are no longer part of the general heritage and need to be reconstructed and revivified in the mind of the reader. But if that suggests that Milton's poems suffer from a special liability, we should remember that even the popular dramatist Shakespeare builds on fundamental ideas which have largely vanished from the modern consciousness and must be reconstructed for full and proper comprehension of the plays. Further, it might be said that, different as Shakespeare and Milton were, their central beliefs and assumptions were similar; the two were infinitely nearer to each other than either is to us. If Milton's religious outlook was puerile or worse, so was Shakespeare's.

We heard Lord David Cecil's complaint that Milton was not really a religious poet because he was a philosopher rather than a devotee. Leaving Milton out of account, we have a sufficient answer to the critic's implied definition of religion in recalling that the Christ of the New Testament was a philosopher rather than a devotee. However, Lord David may be said to have bumped upon a central fact, that Milton was one of the philosophic minds which in all centuries, and not least in the seventeenth, have been the main strength of Christianity. To Milton and many of his philosophic contemporaries we might apply some words of Mr. Eliot's written with reference to the present:

The Idea of a Christian Society is one which we can accept or reject; but if we are to accept it, we must treat Christianity with a great deal more *intellectual* respect than is our wont; we must treat it as being for the individual a matter primarily of thought and not of feeling. The consequences of such an attitude are too serious to be acceptable to everybody: for when the Christian faith is not only felt, but thought, it has practical results which may be inconvenient.[1]

The kind of intellectual and thoughtful attitude which Mr. Eliot stresses as a modern need is for him and others a prime reason for disliking Milton—although we might expect moderns to have at least as much respect for Milton's independence as for Donne's conventional orthodoxy. Moreover, Milton was through most of his career inspired, even more than other Puritans, by a vision of the holy community which makes Mr. Eliot's idea of a Christian society, high and earnest as that is, look a little pallid.

We are not concerned here with Milton's treatment of contemporary problems of religious, civil, and political liberty. The general principles from which his ideas sprang are most familiar in the two pamphlets of 1644, *Of Education* and *Areopagitica*, and most mature and explicit in the large Latin treatise on Christian doctrine; over this last Milton worked for many years in an effort both to clarify his own beliefs and also, apparently, to construct a platform on which Protestants in general could unite. We shall observe only a few things in the three works which have an especially important bearing upon the late poems.

---

[1] *The Idea of a Christian Society* (London: Faber and Faber, 1939), p. 8; (New York: Harcourt, Brace, 1940), pp. 4–5.

The letter on education, looked at horizontally, takes its place with other Puritan pamphlets attacking traditional scholastic studies and modes of teaching and urging practical and empirical reforms. Looked at vertically, the letter appears as one of the last in the long series of Renaissance tracts expounding the educational theory of Christian humanism. Although, like other progressive Puritans, Milton gives a considerable space to science, the main body of material is the ancient classics. These provide much of the necessary literature of knowledge and they nourish all human capacities, especially the faculty of moral choice which leads to rational virtue. But Milton makes it very clear that the highest natural wisdom of the pagans is a subordinate auxiliary of the Bible, that it lacks the special inspiration and final authority of Christian faith and precept. He gives two definitions of education and both are typical of European humanism. The more familiar one is this: "I call therefore a complete and generous education, that which fits a man to perform justly, skilfully, and magnanimously all the offices, both private and public, of peace and war." The less familiar but even more truly Miltonic one is this: "The end then of learning is to repair the ruins of our first parents by regaining to know God aright, and out of that knowledge to love him, to imitate him, to be like him, as we may the nearest by possessing our souls of true virtue, which being united to the heavenly grace of faith, makes up the highest perfection." That is rather remote from the modern educationist's talk about adaptation to environment.

Those who have absorbed the kind of education described in this letter are worthy to enjoy, and must not be

deprived of, the kind of liberty described in *Areopagitica.*
This most famous of Milton's pamphlets, which attracted
no attention in its own day, has long been regarded as one
of the few great declarations of civil liberty in the language. There is no need of rehearsing the arguments, sublime or satirical, but I must read some central passages of
force and beauty which recall the spirit of those days of
confident idealism and partly anticipate the ethical theme
of *Paradise Lost:*

I cannot praise a fugitive and cloistered virtue unexercised
and unbreathed, that never sallies out and sees her adversary,
but slinks out of the race, where that immortal garland is to
be run for, not without dust and heat. Assuredly we bring
not innocence into the world, we bring impurity much
rather; that which purifies us is trial, and trial is by what
is contrary. That virtue therefore which is but a youngling
in the contemplation of evil, and knows not the utmost that
vice promises to her followers, and rejects it, is but a blank
virtue, not a pure; her whiteness is but an excremental whiteness; which was the reason why our sage and serious poet
Spenser, (whom I dare be known to think a better teacher
than Scotus or Aquinas,) describing true temperance under
the person of Guion, brings him in with his palmer through
the cave of Mammon, and the bower of earthly bliss, that he
might see and know, and yet abstain. . . .

Many there be that complain of divine Providence for suffering Adam to transgress. Foolish tongues! when God gave
him reason, he gave him freedom to choose, for reason is but
choosing; he had been else a mere artificial Adam, such an
Adam as he is in the motions. We ourselves esteem not of that
obedience, or love, or gift, which is of force; God therefore
left him free, set before him a provoking object ever almost

in his eyes; herein consisted his merit, herein the right of his reward, the praise of his abstinence. Wherefore did he create passions within us, pleasures round about us, but that these rightly tempered are the very ingredients of virtue? . . .

This justifies the high providence of God, who, though he command us temperance, justice, continence, yet pours out before us even to a profuseness all desirable things, and gives us minds that can wander beyond all limit and satiety.

The general argument of *Areopagitica* is in accord with the ideals of progressive Puritanism, and it is besides everywhere enlarged and enriched by its author's classical culture and humane breadth of view. But two things are not always remembered by libertarians who associate Milton with the principle of complete freedom of speech. One is that his passionate faith in the right of discussion, the power of truth, and the dignity and freedom of individual man carries with it the religious responsibility of individual discipline. The second is that, while maintaining a broad measure of freedom and tolerance, Milton does not leave without safeguards the fundamental and unquestionable bases of religion and morality, and does not object to judicious censorship of dangerous books after publication. If we are disappointed by that, let us remember that the modern right of free speech is in no small degree the result of general scepticism about absolute truth and authority, a kind of scepticism almost unknown in Milton's time and country.

The source and sanction of Milton's ideas of freedom was the Reformation doctrine of Christian liberty, of which he was in seventeenth-century England the greatest among many exponents.[2] This conception is set forth fully in the treatise on Christian doctrine and briefly near the end of *Paradise Lost*, and it is more or less explicit or implicit in nearly all his mature writings. In a word, the Mosaic law was not only positive and truly religious and moral but also restrictive, arbitrary, and ceremonial; it was a precise external code imposed upon man. When Christ came, the Mosaic law was abrogated for the law of the gospel. With his soul illuminated by a new revelation, man was released from his involuntary subjection to the Mosaic law and became, through divine grace and his own insight and effort, a free agent, a self-directing son of God. Regenerate man is in fact freed from dependence upon and allegiance to all external authorities and institutions. The seeds of revolution latent in this Protestant individualism are obvious. Properly understood, of course, the doctrine does not make man irresponsible; it vastly heightens his responsibility to God. Over and over again Milton repeats that liberty is not license, that true liberty can be enjoyed only by the wise and good—and they, as he was driven more and more to recognize, are a minority of mankind.

With this dynamic and individualistic, yet very exacting, principle of Christian liberty is bound up another cardinal principle, that of "right reason," *recta ratio*. This Stoic concept had so long been a part of Christian thought that its origin could be half-forgotten, but it revealed its

---

[2] See A. S. P. Woodhouse's "Milton, Puritanism, and Liberty," *University of Toronto Quarterly*, IV (1935), 483–513, and *Puritanism and Liberty* (London: Dent, 1938), and Arthur Barker's fuller development of these ideas in his *Milton and the Puritan Dilemma* (Toronto: University of Toronto Press, 1942).

classical character, when set against evangelical Christianity, in its emphasis on divine and human reason. The concept was the basic element of Christian humanism in all ages, and in seventeenth-century England Milton was again its greatest exponent, along with the group of Cambridge Platonists.

Right reason is not merely reason in our sense of the word; it is not a dry light, a nonmoral instrument of inquiry. Neither is it simply the religious conscience. It is a kind of rational and philosophic conscience which distinguishes man from the beasts and which links man with man and with God. This faculty was implanted by God in all men, Christian and heathen alike, as a guide to truth and conduct. Though its effectual workings may be obscured by sin, it makes man, in his degree, like God; it enables him, within limits, to understand the purposes of a God who is perfect reason as well as perfect justice, goodness, and love. Hence the ancient pagans, to whom the evangelical Christian is indifferent or hostile, are for the Christian humanist men who achieved very positive steps toward ultimate truth and virtue. Though even the highest pagan wisdom, like Plato's, was the product of only the natural reason, and must be fortified and illuminated by Christian revelation and love, that natural reason was itself a divine gift and it sought the true light. Since all truth is one, since man and the universe and God are rational, the human reason is an ally, not an enemy, of Christianity. Thus the Christian father Lactantius, quoting Cicero's assertion that morality is founded on the eternal law of right reason written in every human heart, could exclaim that the utterance was well-nigh inspired. Thus

37

Erasmus could declare that there were perhaps more saints than those named in the calendar and could add that unforgettable phrase, "*Sancte Socrates, ora pro nobis.*" Thus Hooker, whose first book is such a magnificent picture of the reign of law and reason in the universe and in the mind of God and man, could affirm: "The general and perpetual voice of men is as the sentence of God himself. For that which all men have at all times learned, Nature herself must needs have taught; and God being the author of Nature, her voice is but his instrument." Thus Jeremy Taylor, who so constantly quoted the ancients, could say that the "Christian Religion in all its moral parts is nothing else but the Law of Nature, and great Reason." Thus Benjamin Whichcote, the seminal mind of Cambridge Platonism, reinterpreted, and established as the sign manual of the group, the biblical phrase "The spirit of man is the candle of the Lord," and insisted that right reason is found wherever true faith is found, that

To go against Reason, is to go against God: it is the self same thing, to do that which the Reason of the Case doth require; and that which God Himself doth appoint: Reason is the Divine Governor of Man's Life; it is the very Voice of God.

And thus Milton, to cite only one utterance, maintains that the unwritten law of God

is no other than that law of nature given originally to Adam, and of which a certain remnant, or imperfect illumination, still dwells in the hearts of all mankind; which, in the regenerate, under the influence of the Holy Spirit, is daily tending towards a renewal of its primitive brightness.

Some elements in this concept of right reason may be dwelt upon a little longer, with special reference to the Cambridge Platonists, since there are so many affinities between them and Milton. One is the divine unity and order of the world and the divine unity of all truth, natural and supernatural. Another is a degree of optimism based on that belief and on belief in the essential goodness of man, a belief very different from the Augustinian, Lutheran, Calvinist, and Hobbesian belief in natural depravity. But this optimism was held very firmly in check by a Christian consciousness of human frailty and sin and the need of grace, and was very different from the scientific and sentimental optimism which was soon to submerge it. Thirdly, in spite of an occasional strain of mysticism, the Cambridge Platonists, like Milton, opposed irrational "enthusiasm" and emphasized the active Christian life lived in a world of evil, the rational and ethical imitation of Christ. Finally, to go no further, the doctrine of right reason predicates certain absolute values of good and evil, reason and unreason. Right reason does not turn away from nature as evil, still less does it set up nature against "artificial" restraints of religion and morality. Both attitudes would be impossible because God and nature are one—which does not mean a pantheistic confusion of creation with the Creator and an irreligious worship of life and flux. What we do have is a fundamental opposition to Calvinism on the one hand and naturalism on the other. The great Elizabethan Calvinist, William Perkins, believing in an arbitrary and inscrutable God, could say that His will "itself is an absolute rule both of justice and reason," so that what He wills "thereupon becomes reasonable and just." And at the other extreme Hobbes affirms that man calls good and evil whatever he seeks to possess or avoid, since there is nothing simply and absolutely good or evil. But for men like Hooker and Taylor and the Cambridge Platonists and Milton, the spirit of man and the revealed word of God together proclaim unshakable absolutes which God Himself, if He could be imagined as having the desire, could not change.

I have stressed this great, central, and traditional doctrine of right reason partly because the anti-Miltonists have evidently never heard of it. To quote Mr. Murry again, since his remarks are both typical and explicit, Milton's "apparent peculiarity is that he is overweeningly confident in the natural man, or at least in the natural reason of man . . . and primarily in his own reason." Presumably Mr. Murry and the others would not complain that Hooker and Taylor and the Cambridge Platonists have an overweening confidence in the natural reason of man, and especially in their own reason, but Milton's exaltation of the religious and ethical concept of right reason becomes evidence of his personal and irreligious pride and egotism! It is a rather quaint fact that the charges our theologians bring against Milton's religious "rationalism" are essentially the same as those brought against Whichcote by his quondam tutor, the Calvinist Anthony Tuckney.

Without going into theological and philosophical subtleties we may observe how these ideas are embodied in *Paradise Lost*, and we may look first at the principal object of censure, the Deity. Many persons find that Deity harshly legal, tyrannical, and repellent, and would apparently prefer, and think Milton should have preferred, a Browningesque Deity who was all Love and nothing else, an infinitely vague and amiable grandfather. As a matter of plain fact, Milton does continually stress the prime power of love in God and man; his avowed theme, the assertion of Eternal Providence, means the assertion of eternal love. But Milton's religion, like that of most great writers and thinkers of his age, was not merely emotional and was never soft. His philosophic mind as well as his imagination and emotions required and responded to a partly philosophic Deity. Hebrew and Christian faith of course supplied the main outlines of an omnipotent and omniscient Creator and Sustainer of the world, a just and merciful Judge and Father. With this are fused other concepts, Platonic, Aristotelian, and Stoic, and, since Milton, like other men, retained something of the Calvinistic temper, we may add the allied idea of absolute sovereignty which was central in Calvinism. But there we come to a point where distinctions are needed and are not always made. Even Sir Herbert Grierson can say that in *Paradise Lost* "the will of God, however arbitrary it may appear, is to be obeyed. *That* is reasonable. Heaven is a totalitarian state." [3] *That* remark is a partial summary of the Calvinistic doctrine—witness William Perkins—which it was Milton's object to repudiate. Milton's position might be summed up in two aphorisms of Whichcote's:

Right and Just is determined, not by the Arbitrary pleasure of him that has Power over us; but by the Nature and Reason of Things.

---

[3] *Milton & Wordsworth* (Cambridge University Press; New York: Macmillan, 1937), p. 117.

God does not, because of his Omnipotency, deal Arbitrarily with us; but according to Right, and Reason: and whatever he does, is therefore Accountable; because Reasonable.

The absolute sovereignty of Milton's God, then, is not the arbitrary and tyrannous sovereignty of absolute will, it is the sovereignty of right reason and the law of nature, a sovereignty comprehended by the uncorrupted right reason of man and accepted not as servitude but as the condition of true freedom. "To follow God and to follow right Reason," says Whichcote, "is all one." God means not only infinite power and infinite love, but rational and natural order in the universe, in society, and above all in the soul of man. Those three realms are all united in the doctrine of the great chain of being which had through many centuries been the framework of man's theocentric view of the world. The hierarchic principle of order and degree linked together all animate beings and inanimate things, God, angels, man, animals, plants, and stones. In giving man his place in that descending or ascending order, cosmic and social, it also gave hierarchic order to man's own faculties and values. Thus while the doctrine provided a metaphysical philosophy, it was far more religious and ethical than scientific. The whole world, visible and invisible, is a divine harmony, as Milton is always proclaiming (often in musical terms), and disturbance of that harmony is at once a sin and a violation of nature. "The ways and dealings of God with his Creatures," to quote Whichcote again, "are all Accountable in a way of Reason; but Sinners vary from the Reason of things; and take upon them to Over-rule what is settled and established from Eternity."

Artistically, no doubt, it would have been better if Milton had relied upon his power of suggestion—

Dark with excessive bright thy skirts appear—

and had not made God a speaking character. Both Divine Reason and Divine Father, in becoming a supreme speaker and actor in an epic, inevitably—though not invariably—become less divine. Whether or not the poet shared our uneasiness, he had a problem. His plan required the denial of Calvinistic determinism and the assertion of man's free will and God's providential justice, love, and grace, and the most authoritative mouthpiece for such doctrines might well seem to be God Himself.

But, whatever the occasional defects in presentation, Milton's concept of God appears more rigorous and forbidding to sentimentalists than it does to people who understand the exalted passion for rational and righteous order which inspired many religious thinkers from Aeschylus and Plato to Spinoza, and which was more or less shared, to go no further than Milton's immediate inheritance and background, by serious writers from Spenser, Hooker, and Shakespeare to the supposedly irreligious Hobbes. Even our few quotations from religious writers, especially Whichcote (whose extant sermons, by the way, apparently date from the Restoration period), might give pause to those who complain of a peculiar hard rationality and lack of "mystery" in Milton's religion. A good many modern critics, in their comments on Milton's Deity, only echo the most unreliable of theologians, Satan. Indeed it would be interesting to hear, from those who abhor the theology of *Paradise Lost,* in what essential respects it differed from the theology of the seventeenth-century Anglican divines. Moreover, while there is of course a gulf between the mind of Milton and the mind of Professor Whitehead, one might ask if such sentences as these, from the great modern metaphysician, do not touch some fundamentals of Milton's thought:

God is the one systematic, complete fact, which is the antecedent ground conditioning every creative act. . . .

The kingdom of heaven is not the isolation of good from evil. It is the overcoming of evil by good. . . .

Every event on its finer side introduces God into the world. Through it his ideal vision is given a base in actual fact to which He provides the ideal consequent, as a factor saving the world from the self-destruction of evil. . . .

He transcends the temporal world, because He is an actual fact in the nature of things. He is not there as derivative from the world; He is the actual fact from which the other formative elements cannot be torn apart.

But equally it stands in his nature that He is the realization of the ideal conceptual harmony by reason of which there is an actual process in the total universe—an evolving world which is actual because there is order.[4]

Milton's Christ, as the Son of Milton's God, has incurred partly similar censure.[5] (In *Paradise Regained,* by the

---

[4] A. N. Whitehead, *Religion in the Making* (New York: Macmillan, 1926), pp. 154 ff.

[5] In *The Fortunes of Falstaff* (Cambridge University Press, 1943; New York: Macmillan, 1944, p. 23), Professor Dover Wilson, speaking of the frequent modern failure to appreciate

way, Christ is much less Lord David Cecil's "austere, unsympathetic classical philosopher" than a humble servant of God looking always for divine guidance.)[6] The anti-Trinitarian view of Christ's inferiority to the Father we may ignore, since this heresy, though distinct in the treatise, was not apparent enough in the poem to be observed by generations of devout readers, and since it is not important for us anyhow, except as an example of Milton's independent thinking. With all his emphasis on reason and moral choice, he is thoroughly orthodox in making Christ the incarnation of divine love and the atonement the great manifestation of that love. So Christ, "in whom the fulness dwells of love divine," the one heavenly being who will undertake the sacrificial mission to earth, is everywhere contrasted with the infernal being whose errand on earth is inspired by pride, hatred, and revenge. But whereas in evangelical Christianity, whether in gospel hymns or the poems of Donne, Christ means "the blood of the Lamb shed for me," for Milton as for other Christian humanists Christ is also, in Jeremy Taylor's phrase, "the great exemplar," or, in the words of Whichcote, "the principle of divine life within us, as well as a Saviour without us." Christ is, therefore, along with His other attributes, virtually identified with right reason. The rebel angels

---

Prince Hal and Henry V as the ideal king, observes parallel misunderstandings in Miltonic criticism, and remarks that Milton's Son of God has been charged with priggishness no less freely than Shakespeare's son of Bolingbroke.

[6] Milton's emphasis on Christ's constant faith and humble obedience is shown by Warner G. Rice, "*Paradise Regained*," *Papers of the Michigan Academy of Science, Arts and Letters*, XXII (1937), 493–503.

> reason for thir Law refuse,
> Right reason for thir Law, and for thir King
> Messiah, who by right of merit Reigns.

Thus the Mediator and Redeemer represents not only divine love but the divine beauty of order in the soul and in the world. And the irresistible power of order, truth, and right is splendidly symbolized in the picture of Christ on the third day of battle:

> forth rush'd with whirl-wind sound
> The Chariot of Paternal Deity,
> Flashing thick flames . . .
> He onward came, far off his coming shone.

Finally, as we should expect, Christ is the Logos of Neoplatonic Christianity and the executive agent of God both in subduing rebellion and in creating the universe and man in accordance with "his great Idea."

The supreme manifestation of right reason is God Himself, and what God is in the world, the macrocosm, reason is in the soul of man, the microcosm. This ethical psychology, the sovereignty of the reason and will over the irrational passions and appetites, may seem very naïve in our day, when psychologists pull habits out of rats, but it was through many centuries the working faith of men not inferior to us in experience, intelligence, and vision; and it was admirably restated a few years ago by Walter Lippmann as a creed which modern man must strive to recover. As it appears in more or less Christianized form in the humanistic tradition, it has a varying Platonic, Aristotelian, or Stoic emphasis. Some English representatives are Spenser and Daniel, Chapman and Greville and Jonson. Although Christian Stoicism is strong in Milton as it is in many men of his time, the strongest emphasis and coloring are Platonic. One could cite many proofs of the Platonic strain in the basic texture of Milton's thought and feeling, but perhaps it is enough to recall the two definitions of education quoted already. The second, which some people would label Puritan, is especially close to the Plato who described the life of the true philosopher as "assimilation to God."

In *Paradise Lost* Milton's justification of the ways of God to men turns on two poles. One, the divine love and grace which once made, and continue to make, regeneration possible, belongs to all Christianity. The other, man's rational freedom of moral choice, belongs more particularly to the tradition of Christian humanism. Just now we are concerned with the latter. Some critics have made much of the arbitrary "tabu" which Adam and Eve transgress and which, they think, deprives Milton's fable of serious interest. Certainly Milton neither could nor would have got rid of the biblical tabu, but, without regarding the story as we regard it, he in every way transformed its primitive scale of values so as to make the experience of Adam and Eve a universal example of the trials and weaknesses of every man and every woman. The story had long been interpreted in terms of ancient ethical dualism (among such interpreters in Milton's own time were Sir Thomas Browne, Henry More, and Thomas Traherne), and Milton's elaboration was both traditional and original. As we shall see more fully later, Eve falls through weakness of reason, Adam through weakness of will, and both

47

violate, not merely a tabu, but the order of nature. When they have sinned, their souls are an unnatural chaos of contending passions:

> For Understanding rul'd not, and the Will
> Heard not her lore, both in subjection now
> To sensual Appetite, who from beneath
> Usurping over sovran Reason claim'd
> Superior sway.

It must be emphasized again that this sovereignty of reason is always presented as the wholly natural order, not, as naturalistic thought would have it, an unnatural restraint, and that it is the overthrow of that sovereignty which is unnatural—a thoroughly Socratic doctrine, by the way.[7]

This is all obvious enough, and one could give an outline of *Paradise Lost* which would make the poem appear, on the ethical plane, as only an application of such ideas of rational liberty as were set forth in Milton's early prose. In comparison with Genesis, Milton's treatment of Adam and Eve is decidedly humanistic and rational, and as such it may not be thought contemptible, even in times when the Bible and Plato have given place to Freud. But what makes, or should make, a stronger appeal is a vital modification of that rational humanism which comes from the soul of an older and sadder and wiser Milton. To put it in the broadest and simplest way, for the author of *Paradise Lost* the great root of all man's sin and evil is pride, his

---

[7] Cf. Whichcote, Aphorism 814: "It is contrary to the order of things; for Will and Affections to go before Understanding and Judgment. It is natural, that Will should follow; and that Understanding should go before."

great need is religious humility. The prohibition of the tree of knowledge is not a mere tabu, it is a test of religious humility, faith, and obedience. In his theological treatise Milton gave a list of the many and various kinds of sin involved in the fall, and the list ended with "presumption in aspiring to divine attributes, fraud in the means employed to attain the object, pride, and arrogance." Sir Herbert Grierson, in developing the view already recorded, that God is the arbitrary ruler of a totalitarian state, says that some use might have been made of the idea of presumption, "But there is no hint of the kind in *Paradise Lost.*" [8] Although Sir Herbert's words seem plain enough, one can hardly believe that one understands them, since pride and presumption are Milton's whole theme.

We shall be looking at the characters and drama later, but we may here glance briefly through the poem and see the main lines on which Milton interprets or reinterprets his fable. The first few books show, dramatically, the great embodiment of pride and presumption defeated but still aspiring to equality with God. The middle books are occupied with the visit of the archangel Raphael, through whom Adam and Eve are given various and repeated warnings, direct and indirect. Very significantly, as Mr. Tillyard observes in his *Elizabethan World Picture* (1943), the first piece of instruction Raphael imparts is an exposition of the great chain of being, the principle of hierarchic order which we noticed a while ago. Then comes the angel's long account of Satan's rebellion against that order and of the war and chaos which symbolize pride

---

[8] *Milton & Wordsworth* (Cambridge University Press; New York: Macmillan, 1937), p. 117.

and presumption running amuck. In contrast with that, there follows the account of Creation, the establishment of divine order and harmony.

By degrees we descend from the cosmic to the human, and warnings against presumption become more direct. In the eighth book we have a scientific discourse prompted by Adam's curiosity about the workings of the universe in which he finds himself. (It was unfortunate that at this point Eve, who as the first sinner was especially in need of counsel, should have obeyed feminine decorum and have left the gentlemen to their high masculine converse; her expectation of receiving a later digest from her husband was not adequately fulfilled.) Raphael explains the alternative theories of a geocentric and heliocentric world and related problems, but Milton's interest is not in astronomy itself, it is in the cautions with which the angel begins and ends, and with which Adam agrees:

> Solicit not thy thoughts with matters hid,
> Leave them to God above, him serve and fear. . . .

> But apt the Mind or Fancy is to rove
> Uncheckt, and of her roving is no end;
> Till warn'd, or by experience taught, she learn
> That not to know at large of things remote
> From use, obscure and subtle, but to know
> That which before us lies in daily life,
> Is the prime Wisdom; what is more is fume,
> Or emptiness, or fond impertinence,
> And renders us in things that most concern
> Unpractis'd, unprepar'd, and still to seek.

Milton is not attacking science as such. In *Paradise Lost* he pays tribute to "the Tuscan artist," Galileo, whom he had celebrated in *Areopagitica* as a martyr to truth. And there is better though indirect evidence in what everyone knows, that Milton's imagination responds, as no other English poet's has responded with equal power, to the conception of infinite space. His words here, then, are not a fundamentalist and obscurantist attack on science any more than Christ's disparagement of Greek culture in *Paradise Regained* represents a barbarous hostility to the classics. In both cases Milton is simply asserting, with an earnestness born of ripened insight, his lifelong hierarchy of values; and his stress on temperance in knowledge, on the proper place and limits of human inquiry, can be paralleled in many other writers of the century, among them Dr. John Donne. There had been in the younger Milton a Baconian strain, which is conspicuous in the letter on education, but it had always been much less central than the ethical and religious. In *The Reason of Church Government* (1641–1642), for instance, he had characteristically distinguished between "that knowledge that rests in the contemplation of natural causes and dimensions, which must needs be a lower wisdom, as the object is low," and "the only high valuable wisdom," the knowledge of God and the ultimate ends of human life. With advancing years and increasing realization of the weakness of the human reason and will, Milton has come more and more to exalt the knowledge, love, and imitation of God and to fear scientific speculation or Greek philosophy or anything else which may obscure or distort man's vision and nourish irreligious pride in his own mind and powers.[9] As he says in the first chapter of the *Christian Doctrine*, "obedience and love are always the best guides to knowledge." "Every man," Thomas à Kempis had said, "naturally desires to know, but of what value is knowledge without the fear of God?"

Astronomical curiosity is only the most obvious example of vain presumption, and when we come to the drama of the fall the motive is generalized. Pride aspiring beyond human limits and human needs, the desire for power through knowledge, is the one motive steadily appealed to throughout Satan's temptation of Eve—in his plan of attack, in the dream he puts into her mind, in his successful dialogue with her, in her soliloquies before and after her sin, and in her subsequent persuading of Adam. If we want any further proof that the theme of *Paradise Lost* is the conflict between human pride and religious humility, we have it in the most significant place, the conclusion. After the archangel Michael has unfolded to Adam the sinful history of the human race, Adam is reconciled to the loss of Eden by the consciousness that he may gain a new Eden within his own soul:

> Greatly instructed I shall hence depart,
> Greatly in peace of thought, and have my fill
> Of knowledge, what this Vessel can contain;

---

[9] It might be observed that the phrase in *Areopagitica*, "minds that can wander beyond all limit and satiety," a phrase used there with recognition of the dangers latent in the exercise of God's great gift, is echoed in *Paradise Lost* (ii, 146–148) by the perverter of reason, Belial.

Beyond which was my folly to aspire.
Henceforth I learn, that to obey is best,
And love with fear the only God, to walk
As in his presence, ever to observe
His providence, and on him sole depend,
Merciful over all his works, with good
Still overcoming evil, and by small
Accomplishing great things, by things deem'd weak
Subverting worldly strong, and worldly wise
By simply meek; that suffering for Truth's sake
Is fortitude to highest victory,
And to the faithful Death the Gate of Life;
Taught this by his example whom I now
Acknowledge my Redeemer ever blest.

And Michael replies with a last reminder of the gulf which separates merely human and scientific knowledge and worldly power from the true knowledge and power that are within:

This having learnt, thou hast attain'd the sum
Of wisdom; hope no higher, though all the Stars
Thou knew'st by name, and all th' ethereal Powers,
All secrets of the deep, all Nature's works,
Or works of God in Heav'n, Air, Earth, or Sea,
And all the riches of this World enjoy'dst,
And all the rule, one Empire; only add
Deeds to thy knowledge answerable, add Faith,
Add Virtue, Patience, Temperance, add Love,
By name to come call'd Charity, the soul
Of all the rest: then wilt thou not be loath
To leave this Paradise, but shalt possess
A paradise within thee, happier far.

This is the message of the poet who, according to Mr. Murry, is "completely emancipated from the humility of religious faith"; [10] who, according to Mr. Leavis, "offers as ultimate for our worship mere brute assertive will"; who, according to Lord David Cecil, lacked the Christian sensibility, did not live by faith, scorned hope, was indisposed to charity, and regarded pride not as a vice but as the mark of a superior nature. If there is in English verse any truer or more deeply felt summary of Christ's teaching than Milton's lines, I do not recall it. Certainly there is no equivalent in the "first" among English Christian poets, John Donne.

Critics who see only one Milton, and him not very clearly, make that disagreeable and unchanging Milton the author of the major poems. They seem to think that, like the younger Pitt, "he never grew, he was cast," and cast in a mould of humanistic arrogance and self-sufficiency. So far as this view is founded on private intuition and the studious ignoring of his works, there is no way to meet it. So far as it is founded on evidence, it seems to be a very hasty and superficial reaction to the ardent and militant optimism which inspired Milton's efforts to forward the great revolution. The author of the early pamphlets was on fire with hope and confidence in the complete and immediate regeneration of England and in time of the world. This pamphleteer and prophet was assuredly religious, if the Hebrew prophets were religious, but he was then on the rising and winning side; his personal faith had not been tested, and in his prose writings it was partly

[10] *Studies in Keats New and Old* (London: Oxford University Press, 1939), p. 110.

submerged in his public themes. But the Milton of *Paradise Lost* and the later poems had undergone a long series of disillusionments. He had lost faith in bishops, king, parliament, people, army, even Cromwell. And then, while *Paradise Lost* was being composed, came the Restoration. His twenty years of service to the good old cause, his eyesight, all his hopes, were gone. At moments he was tempted to despair even of God's providence. But in spite of many defeats he was not conquered,

> though fall'n on evil days,
> On evil days though fall'n, and evil tongues;
> In darkness, and with dangers compast round,
> And solitude.

What emerged now, in his last poems, was a more truly religious faith, not attached to and partly dependent upon dreams of a new era, but founded only upon God and the soul of individual man. Milton has not abandoned the principles of Christian liberty and right reason, because these are fundamental, but he has a new understanding of the divine nature and of human nature. The aggressive reformer has arrived at the full realization that "in His will is our peace." That is the one great text of his last three poems.

The evolution of Milton's thought and feeling, the deepening of his spiritual insight, makes him very much our contemporary. If he were as actively present to our minds as he should be, modern writers would have been pointing to the megalomaniac Satan and his destructive energy as a superlative prophetic picture of the world conquerors of our time. The word "prophetic" is not used, to be sure, in a literal sense; but neither is the parallel merely fortuitous. For the traditional motives which, with Milton's special coloring and emphasis, led to the sin of Satan and Adam and Eve, are the essential motives which have been seen at the root of the sickness of our civilization. One could not begin to catalogue the modern authors, not only philosophic but semipopular, who have been analyzing the rise and the downfall of the so-called "Renaissance man." (The term "Renaissance" in this connection is, I think, partly a misnomer, because the central Renaissance tradition was predominantly Christian, but there is no doubt concerning the rebellious mentality and movement so designated, that is, secular, self-sufficient, optimistic "liberalism.") These modern authors, looking back from the present chaos over the last three centuries, have, like Milton, seen man's undoing in his irreligious human pride. It was in Milton's own age that advanced minds in Europe generally, even if not irreligious themselves, made the first thorough break with the religious world view and religious ethics of the Middle Ages and antiquity and inaugurated the scientific naturalism and scientific *hybris* of modern times. Milton's own career might be called a partial epitome of that long cycle; if he began with a measure of "humanistic" self-sufficiency, he ended with repudiating it. In *Paradise Lost*, setting fundamental motives in the clear relief of an ancient author, Milton showed the will to power, public and private, intellectual presumption, and egoistic desire, seeking their ends through force and fraud and overthrowing the divine and natural order in the world and in the soul. He surveyed a world going through pride to destruction and issued a serious call to a devout and holy life.

The same words, however inadequate for both poems, might be used of *The Waste Land*, the nearest thing we have to a modern *Paradise Lost*. And are not those critics who dismiss Milton's purpose and theme and substance inclined to demand more of him than they do of other poets? Has not *The Waste Land*, with all the advantages of contemporaneity, suffered much the same fate as *Paradise Lost?* We are thrilled by its magical phrases and rhythms, we track down the sources of allusions, and we place the work in the poet's religious development, but has it actually counted very much in our own? Has it in the least shaken our natural pride and led us to repentance, or does any critic call it a failure because it has not? And is not its "message" as much "out of date" as Milton's? But Mr. Eliot, except as a technician, stands apart from the modern movement, and the modern temper has been formed largely by writers who have attained a foggy pinnacle beyond good and evil. That is one prime reason for reading Milton. We need the shock of encountering a poet to whom good and evil are distinct realities, a poet who has a much-tried but invincible belief in a divine order and in man's divine heritage and responsibility, who sees in human life an eternal contest between irreligious pride and religious humility.

III

CHARACTERS AND DRAMA

W<small>E HAVE CONSIDERED</small> some of the positive values embodied in Milton's God and Christ, and have seen something of the way in which those values are violated by Satan and by Adam and Eve. We may now, with apologies for occasional repetition or elaboration, look more closely at the sinners themselves and at Milton's methods of presenting the conflict between good and evil.

In his general pattern Milton naturally followed ancient and modern epic tradition (he could hardly be expected to have conceived the irregular method of *The Waste Land*), but he expressly rejected the traditional kind of material. *Paradise Lost* is by far the most important survivor of the many heroic poems which were being written all over Europe in the seventeenth century, so that it is often regarded as a solitary and peculiarly Puritan work. But Milton's choice of a biblical subject was in full accord with the European movement, since the effect of both the Reformation and the Counter Reformation had been to turn epic ambitions away from secular to Christian material. Milton himself had early contemplated a British subject, which would of course have been Christian, but he settled on one of much broader and deeper significance, one which had already attracted other European poets.

When we compare Milton's poem with the ancient epics, we see that his subject involved special difficulties, difficulties of a kind apparent to some degree in Virgil. These are mostly comprised in one large fact, the widening gulf between material and theme. In Homer material and theme were indivisible; all the spiritual values of life were concentrated in the active courage of the warrior and the traveler in a dark world of flux and futility. The *Aeneid*, however, moves on more than one level, and we feel a partial disharmony between the prescribed pattern of war and voyaging, the traditional stuff of the epic, and the abstract theme. And Virgil's abstract theme is not single. It obviously presents the glory of the Italian past and the Italian destiny. But in a larger way it presents what C. S. Lewis has called "a transition in the world-order, the shift of civilization from the East to the West, the transformation of the little remnant, the *reliquias*, of the old, into the germ of the new." [1] And, thirdly, there is the more positively religious and ethical idea of a pilgrim's progress; Aeneas is led, through trial and suffering, by divine providence and a sense of duty. The second and third of these themes may be said to have their parallels in Milton's poem. But a concrete pattern and material already inadequate for the philosophic Virgil were not less so for a poet of the seventeenth century, and the gulf between Milton's material and his theme was increased by the special nature of his fable. That fable was, for most men of his century, a record of one of the two

[1] *A Preface to* Paradise Lost (London: Oxford University Press, 1942), pp. 34–35.

greatest events in the history of the world and, as I said, it had attracted other poets, but as characters it had of course only supernatural beings and two scarcely normal human beings. The wonder is not that Milton did not overcome all his problems but that he triumphantly overcame so many of them. One of Mr. Eliot's most quoted asides is this: "Milton's celestial and infernal regions are large but insufficiently furnished apartments filled by heavy conversation; and one remarks about the Puritan mythology its thinness." [2] Well, a critic with as little sympathy for Dante as Mr. Eliot has for Milton might say that *The Divine Comedy* presents a small but crowded prison and a somewhat gloomy visitor's painful interviews with the convicts, which are happily concluded by a chat with the Warden's daughter. Milton's insufficiently furnished apartments contain the marvelous pictures of hell and of vast space, and the heavy conversation includes the defiant speeches of Satan and the greatly dramatic debate in Pandemonium. And the "thin" story of Satan and Adam and Eve was not a Puritan invention. Indeed there is very little of the specifically Puritan in *Paradise Lost* or in the whole body of Milton's poetry.

The poet's consciousness of at least some of his problems is made clear by the repeated apologies put into the mouth of Raphael when he tells Adam of the war in heaven and the Creation:

> and what surmounts the reach
> Of human sense, I shall delineate so,

[2] *Selected Essays* (London: Faber and Faber, 1932), p. 307; (New York: Harcourt, Brace, 1932), p. 279.

By lik'ning spiritual to corporal forms,
As may express them best, though what if Earth
Be but the shadow of Heav'n, and things therein
Each to other like, more than on earth is thought?

Often we cannot be sure at what point in his own mind
Milton distinguished the imaginative and symbolic from
what he and his age regarded as historical. That he allowed
himself a large license is amply evident when we put
Paradise Lost beside the *Christian Doctrine* and find, for
example, that in the treatise only a few lines are given to
Satan and little more to the revolt of the angels and the
war in heaven. This last episode is a good illustration of
the difficulty of handling abstract ideas in the concrete
terms of the traditional epic. The long account of the war
is a picture of ambitious pride attempting to overthrow
righteousness and order and bringing about utter chaos
and destruction. As a whole it is done with imaginative
power and energy such as only Milton can command, yet
in parts it is too unreal for an epic, in parts too realistic for
a symbol. Another example might be God's proclamation
of Christ as Messiah, the event which inflames Satan to
revolt. The situation is the same as that in *Macbeth* when
Macbeth is aroused by Duncan's nomination of Malcolm
as heir-apparent. But Milton is not making God into a
human and dynastically minded king, still less is he giving
a philosophic explanation of the origin of evil; he is
establishing Christ in His place as the Son of God, the
Mediator between God and man, the active agent of good
in the world. The nature and necessities of epic narrative,
however, convert a spiritual symbol into a concrete
dramatic incident.

But we must turn from generalities to the characters. Bestriding our path is the colossal figure of Satan, who has misled not only a host of angels and Adam and Eve but a host of critics as well. Since the romantic age, which misinterpreted a number of great works, it has been conventional to regard Satan as the real hero of *Paradise Lost.* We can readily understand how revolutionary poets like Blake and Shelley could make over Milton in their own image; what is less understandable is the persistence of that attitude. And, though Miltonic scholars are not likely to be taken in, the Satanist fallacy is by no means confined to popular opinion. Instead of citing various modern literary critics, I will simply mention such an official compendium as the most widely used history of English literature (1924 ff.), that of Émile Legouis and Louis Cazamian—and, to be very up-to-date, the latest short history (1943) by two English scholars.[3] To quote one

---

[3] W. J. Entwistle and E. Gillett, *The Literature of England, A.D. 500–1942* (London: Longmans, Green, 1943), p. 71. See Legouis and Cazamian, English translation (New York: Macmillan, 1940), pp. 603–604. One refreshing exception to the general rule is George Sampson, *Concise Cambridge History of English Literature* (Cambridge University Press; New York: Macmillan, 1941), pp. 368–369.

Mr. G. Rostrevor Hamilton's *Hero or Fool? A Study of Milton's Satan* (London: Allen and Unwin, 1944) is largely a restatement of the usual romantic view of a dichotomy between Milton the passionate creator and Milton the moralistic commentator. With all his perceptiveness, Mr. Hamilton—whose reference to Prometheus (p. 37) suggests Shelleyan rather than Aeschylean sympathies—does not seem to understand that a poet can be, or could be, passionate in his celebration of Law and Order.

representative judgment, in a survey of the literature of the English Renaissance (1938), Professor Pinto writes in this fashion:

> In Milton's hands the primitive Hebrew myth is transformed into a symbol of the consciousness of his own age. The tremendous figure of Satan (who does not even appear in Genesis) comes to represent in *Paradise Lost* the untamed and passionate will of the individual in revolt against a God who is no longer the personal deity of the Hebrews, but the abstract Reason or First Cause of philosophy. . . . "It is," as Professor Lascelles Abercrombie has written, "in the figure of Satan that the imperishable significance of *Paradise Lost* is centred." All the indomitable heroism of the Puritan armies finds expression in his defiance:

> > What though the field be lost?
> > All is not lost; the unconquerable Will,
> > And study of revenge, immortal hate,
> > And courage never to submit or yield:
> > And what is else not to be overcome?

But it is more than the tragedy of Milton and his friends that is expressed in *Paradise Lost*. It is the tragedy of the modern world, the conflict of the individual will in revolt against the determinism of an inexorable fate. Milton expressed that conflict, but the nature of the mythology to which he was bound prevented him from resolving it, at any rate, on the poetic plane, though he attempted to do so on the plane of argument by means of the elaborate pantheistic system of his Latin *De Doctrina Christiana*. Blake's words remain the profoundest comment on the antinomy that troubles every thoughtful reader of *Paradise Lost*, however much he may admire the splendour of its art:

. . . The reason Milton wrote in fetters when he wrote of

angels and God, and at liberty when of devils and Hell is because he was a true poet and of the Devil's party without knowing it.[4]

Except for particular allusions, we might be reading, say, a critique of Byron's *Cain*. When a specialist in seventeenth-century literature can so interpret Milton, we need not invoke less learned witnesses to prove that the romantic notion of Satan still flourishes. And it is not a small matter, for our whole view of the poem and the poet turns on it.

The argument is in brief that, since God is so unpleasant and Satan is a being of such magnificent vitality, Milton, in spite of his consciously different purpose, must have put his heart and soul into the projection of Satan. We might find a partial parallel in the *Aeneid,* in which, we are often told, the stuffy nominal hero is greatly overshadowed by a character with whom we were not intended to sympathize. For many readers, especially for those who, like many readers of *Paradise Lost,* know only the first few books, Virgil's most vital and central figure is Dido. She alone is humanly and tragically real, while Aeneas, the embodiment of Roman virtue, and Jupiter, Divine Providence, are, like Milton's Adam and God, pallid, self-righteous, and irritating. To persons of this way of thinking, or feeling, there seems to be a central discord in both poems, a conflict between the poet's intention and the result. Both Dido and Satan, it appears, are much too great and attractive for their functional role as villains.

---

[4] *The English Renaissance, 1510–1688* (London: Cresset Press; New York: Robert M. McBride, 1938), pp. 112–113.

But Dido would certainly have been an ineffectual villain if she had not had magnetism enough to charm Aeneas (and us), and Satan would certainly have been an ineffectual villain if he had not had magnetism enough to sway a host of followers (and us). To put the case in that manner, though, might suggest that Virgil and Milton sat down to calculate in cold blood how much vitality they could allow such characters and made a mistake in their arithmetic. The notion sounds much better in this form—that Virgil and Milton had it in their heads to set forth certain orthodox principles but were carried away unwittingly by their hearts and imaginations. No doubt artists have sometimes produced effects different from what they intended, have produced works with internal antinomies, but if any artists in the world have given the impression of knowing what they are about, it is Virgil and Milton. That these poets should in their major works reveal a fundamental religious and moral contradiction one may find it quite impossible to conceive.

But let us glance at a clearer case, at a poet much closer in time and outlook to Milton. When we come upon the speeches in which Iago, Edmund, Macbeth, and the rest concoct their diabolical plans against the good, do we exclaim, "Here is the real Shakespeare, the poet who was of the devil's party without knowing it?" No one disputes the vitality of these great villains, but one doubts if even the most crackbrained of Shakespearian critics, and there are many, have ever suggested that Shakespeare was at heart an Iago or Edmund or Macbeth who forgot his principles in creating such congenial characters. And Shakespeare is only one of the multitude of serious authors who have treated serious themes and created great bad characters in the process. Were all these authors on the side of evil, or is Milton to be the solitary victim of an astonishing naïveté?

Of course it is said, with a romantic transmutation of values, that Satan is really "right," and that brings us to deeper and more disastrous reasons for the misunderstanding of Milton. We can indeed see the same reasons at work in the interpretation of Shakespeare, even if it stops short of the palpable absurdities just imagined. Mr. Eliot, who may be cited as an influential representative of many, appears to sum up Shakespeare's philosophy as "the mixed and muddled scepticism of the Renaissance." [5] Students of Renaissance thought, however, would say that, no matter how far and wide Shakespeare's imagination traveled, his plays were solidly built on the traditional Renaissance orthodoxy of order and degree in the soul, in society, and in the cosmos. And that same orthodoxy, developed with more philosophic learning and more positive religous zeal, is central in Milton. The fact is simply that the modern world has moved quite away from the old assumptions and doctrines of religious, ethical, social, and cosmic order and right reason. It is perhaps a fair guess that among the general reading public three out of four persons instinctively sympathize with any character who suffers and rebels, and pay little heed to the moral values and responsibilities involved, because in such cases the sinner is always right and authority and rectitude

---

[5] *Selected Essays* (London: Faber and Faber, 1932), p. 137; (New York: Harcourt, Brace, 1932), p. 117.

are always wrong. We have much more sympathy with *virtù*, which is always exciting, than with virtue, which is always smug. This instinctive response has of course grown the stronger as religion and morality have been increasingly sapped by romantic naturalism and sentimentalism. So thoroughly are we debauched by these flabby "liberal" doctrines that when we encounter an artist who passionately affirms the laws of justice, reason, and righteousness, the laws that grow not old, we cannot understand his high convictions and purposes and either turn from them in disgust or explain them away. The moment such principles are associated with a poet, he becomes automatically a timid and conventional reactionary or, in the case of Milton, too simple-minded to understand human experience. To celebrate Milton therefore as the great champion of a religious and ethical orthodoxy is to bring ignominy upon him. As Hooker said in opening his defense of divine and human reason against dogmatic and irrational Calvinism, a rebel always finds a ready and admiring audience, whereas one who maintains things established has to meet a number of heavy prejudices. And Milton, the great Puritan enemy of the Anglican church, was in the same tradition of Christian humanism as Hooker.

But, it may be asked, what then becomes of the bold rebel and pamphleteer against ecclesiastical and civil authority? Certainly Milton was a great rebel, on one plane, but on another he was not, and it is fatal to ignore the difference. Milton was a rebel like his own Abdiel, the faithful angel whom Satan could not seduce and who received from God the noble praise:

> Servant of God, well done, well hast thou fought
> The better fight, who single hast maintain'd
> Against revolted multitudes the Cause
> Of Truth, in word mightier than they in Arms;
> And for the testimony of Truth hast borne
> Universal reproach, far worse to bear
> Than violence: for this was all thy care
> To stand approv'd in sight of God, though Worlds
> Judg'd thee perverse.

Or one might think of such a "rebellious" servant of God as Socrates, who has also suffered sometimes from the charge of personal arrogance. For the modern "liberal," knowing no absolute imperatives and having no beliefs, in the old meaning of the word, can think of no explanation except arrogant self-righteousness for the inward strength, "Unshak'n, unseduc'd, unterrifi'd," of one to whom life means obedience to God.

The many readers who glorify Satan of course regard Milton's God as an almighty King Charles, a tyrant against whom it was glorious to rebel. I trust that that wild notion has been exploded by what was said before about Milton's conception of God as the supreme source and symbol of love, mercy, justice, reason, and order. For an eloquent summary of that conception I may quote the last words of Hooker's first book:

Wherefore that here we may briefly end: of Law there can be no less acknowledged, than that her seat is the bosom of God, her voice the harmony of the world: all things in heaven and earth do her homage, the very least as feeling her care, and the greatest as not exempted from her power, both Angels and men and creatures of what condition soever, though each in different sort and manner, yet all with uniform consent, admiring her as the mother of their peace and joy.

This is the sacred and sublime law, the divine harmony, that Satan seeks to overthrow.

The common fallacy begins with a basic misapprehension of the beginning of *Paradise Lost*, namely, Satan's first speech delivered as he surveys his followers rolling in the fiery gulf, confounded though immortal. Before we look at the speech we may remind ourselves that Milton's dramatic methods are much the same as those of the Elizabethan playwrights. In a soliloquy uttered later on his way to Eden—a soliloquy originally written, we are told, as the first speech for the drama Milton had planned —Satan condemns himself with a thoroughness which even God could hardly amplify. Such an open avowal of wickedness by a villain we may assign to the naïve plane of dramaturgy, though we have it everywhere in Shakespeare and his fellows. But the dramatists, and Milton, also use a more dramatic and sophisticated method. They contrive a speech in such terms that, without being a direct confession of evil, it will be so opposed to accepted ideas and values as to invite condemnation by the audience; and that desired response may also be guided through the reaction of a character of recognized goodness. Milton's narrative and descriptive medium encouraged still more direct guidance of our response, though he too could use purely dramatic irony without comment.

In the case of this first speech, our response is prepared

for through the picture of the archangel torn by wholly evil passions. But even if there were no such preparation, the speech itself in every line should arouse horror and repulsion. It is a dramatic revelation of nothing but egoistic pride and passion, of complete spiritual blindness. The "Potent Victor in his rage" is a blind and blasphemous description of God. Nothing that that Victor can inflict will make Satan "repent or change." This phrase, which Shelley remembered as glorious at the end of *Prometheus Unbound*, is a repudiation of all Christian teaching; and one might quote Lord Vansittart on the Germans' national fallacy that only the weak repent. Satan's "injur'd merit" is a figment of his own egoism, quite the opposite of the real and selfless merit of Christ.

> What though the field be lost?
> All is not lost. . . .

These famous lines embody, not the spirit of the Puritan armies, but the spirit of Hitler. Satan sees only a conflict between himself, the world conqueror, and a temporarily superior force; he cannot see that it is a conflict between evil and good. "The unconquerable Will" is not the religious and ethical will, it is the irreligious and naturalistic will to power. "Study of revenge" and "immortal hate" brand themselves.

> Courage never to submit or yield

is not true courage, it is the courage of a wolf at bay, of Hitler again, desperate perseverance in evil. In short, if we think defiance is splendid, regardless of what is defied, if

70

we read this speech with a thrill of sympathy, we ought to feel the same thrill in reading the speeches of Iago and Edmund and Macbeth. Certainly Milton did no less than Shakespeare to guide our reaction. But anything is possible to romantic sentimentalism combined with indifference to the principles on which Milton, like Shakespeare, stood. Even Walter Savage Landor, a romantic revolutionary and neopagan who loathed Milton's theology, could see that "There is neither truth nor wit . . . in saying that Satan is hero of the piece, unless, as is usually the case in human life, he is the greatest hero who gives the widest sway to the worst passions."

I have dwelt on this first speech of Satan's because, as I said, it is for so many readers and critics the beginning of error. There is no antinomy here between Milton's intention and the result, and there is none later, even when he leaves dramatic speech to create its own effect. Those who admire the rebel of the first speech also admire him when he declares:

> Here at least
> We shall be free. . . .
> To reign is worth ambition though in Hell:
> Better to reign in Hell, than serve in Heav'n.

But to those who comprehend and feel Milton's principles, which are everywhere made clear, such words tell how far Satan is from understanding true liberty, how far slavery to pride and passion is from Him in whose service is perfect freedom. Or take the great moment when Satan, his face entrenched with deep scars of thunder, surveys the host he has led to ruin and can hardly speak:

Thrice he assay'd, and thrice in spite of scorn,
Tears such as Angels weep, burst forth: at last
Words interwove with sighs found out thir way.

If, again, one has an impulse to admire a powerful leader momentarily remorseful in defeat, one may think of Hitler explaining his later campaigns. Satan is of course a far grander figure than Hitler, but their motives are closely parallel. In fact Milton uses what was for the sixteenth and seventeenth centuries the equivalent of Hitler in repeatedly likening Satan to a Sultan; Richard Knolles in 1603 had summed up western feeling when he began his history with the phrase "The glorious empire of the Turks, the present terror of the world." The tyrant of Milton's poem, as some readers have seen, is not God but Satan.

Of course Satan has heroic qualities. A character of Mr. Aldous Huxley's remarks: "Indeed, you can't be really bad unless you *do* have most of the virtues. Look at Milton's Satan for example. Brave, strong, generous, loyal, prudent, temperate, self-sacrificing. And let's give the dictators the credit that's due to them; some of them are nearly as virtuous as Satan. Not quite, I admit, but nearly. That's why they can achieve so much evil." [6] And if Satan has heroic virtues, so has Macbeth. Both characters possess the emotional advantage—if we do not feel the values involved—of fighting against odds, while the representatives of goodness and right have irresistible power. The situation is in fact essentially the same. Satan

---

[6] *After Many a Summer Dies the Swan* (London: Chatto and Windus, 1939), p. 115; (New York: Harper, 1939), p. 130.

is overthrown when Christ is armed with the might of God; Macbeth, who has leagued himself with the powers of Satan, is overthrown by the English army, which is, says Malcolm, the instrument of the powers above. Both poets, though imaginatively capable of creating a great villain, are constrained by their traditional faith in Providence and the ultimate triumph of good to bring divine power to the defeat of evil—which is not to say that Shakespeare and Milton always saw good triumphant here and now—and, compared with the dauntless archangel and the bloody tyrant at bay, Christ and Malcolm may not win much of our sympathy.[7] But to revert again to a more immediately conclusive example, whatever sentimental aberrations may cloud the minds of readers of poetry, few countries or persons seem to be filled with sympathetic admiration for Germany because it has been fighting bravely against the three strongest powers of the world.

Satan's first speech has proclaimed him a great outlaw, a Titan of the Hebrew and Christian cosmogony, and his spiritual state receives concrete illustration in the loss of his archangelic grandeur when he arrives in Eden to pursue his campaign against man. He is compared with a wolf and he takes the actual shape of various creatures,

---

[7] In speaking of *Macbeth* and *Paradise Lost*, one might add that the discussion between Malcolm and Macduff, concerning the wicked and the ideal king, is commonly regarded by modern readers as a curious layer of unpoetic dullness, and as such it may be linked with Milton's council in heaven; for the modern reader does not share the traditional convictions about divine, public, and individual order on which both passages are based.

finally a toad and a serpent. But these bestial transforma-
tions are less interesting than his metamorphosis into a
very human villain. At his first sight of Adam and Eve in
their blissful innocence he can indulge in the sardonic
humor of Richard III:

> League with you I seek,
> And mutual amity so strait, so close,
> That I with you must dwell, or you with me
> Henceforth.

Witnessing the two

> Imparadis't in one another's arms,

he feels the sensual sting of Iago or Leontes. Later he ap-
proaches Eve with the flattering guile of Iachimo.

But we must leave Satan and observe the far more
elaborate humanizing process in Milton's treatment of
Adam and Eve. As we first see them, they are ideal man
and ideal woman, ideal husband and ideal wife, wholly
happy in their relations with each other and with God, liv-
ing in a natural world of eternal spring and incomparable
beauty. One line, by the way, in Milton's first picture of
them,

> Hee for God only, shee for God in him,

has evoked both mirth and annoyance; but it simply
embodies the hierarchical view of order and degree
which, as we have seen, was a universal heritage, and
which Shakespeare appealed to at the end of *The Taming
of the Shrew.*

The place of right reason in Milton's conception of

man and life and God is nowhere more strikingly illustrated than in his account of love between man and
woman. This has been regarded, with favor or otherwise,
as the Puritan ideal of marriage set forth in a versified
Puritan conduct book. The Puritan ideal was certainly
not low, nor ascetic, but Milton's ideal has some distinctive
characteristics. For one thing, he is decidedly more
emphatic and outspoken than most Puritans in exalting
the physical expression and enrichment of love. The im-
portance he gives to "Love's due Rites" has a metaphysical basis, namely, his belief in the essential oneness
of matter and spirit, yet this emphasis is part of, and not
at odds with, his larger emphasis on the rational nature of
human love. True love, as opposed to sensual passion, is

> Founded in Reason, Loyal, Just, and Pure.

It

> is the scale
> By which to heav'nly Love thou may'st ascend.

Even

> smiles from Reason flow,
> To brute deni'd, and are of Love the food,
> Love not the lowest end of human life.

If to us such phrases sound starched and chilling, it is because we do not understand and do not feel the positive
and emotional values contained in the idea of reason.

When Milton turns from the cosmic to the human
stage, epic technique largely gives place to intimate drama.
An elaborate chain of incident and motive leads up to the
fall. Readers who find Adam and Eve somewhat stodgy

in their idyllic pastoral happiness must have missed the tragic irony through which the pair are viewed. Milton's description of primeval beauty, harmony, love, and joy is not mere exuberance, it comes after Satan has entered the garden; the contrast between present and future indeed draws expressions of pity not only from the poet but from the malignant tempter. Many passages which may seem to be merely idyllic have their dramatic value. Eve's account of her first moments of existence and her first meeting with Adam gives, through veiled adaptations of the myths of Narcissus and of Apollo and Daphne, the first hint of her vanity and of his passion. Later Satan, planning his campaign, decides that, since Adam and Eve are happy in humble ignorance and obedience, he will kindle an ambitious desire for superhuman knowledge. In the fancy of the sleeping Eve he forges a dream which, in great distress, she tells Adam when she is awakened. An angel, she dreamed, had persuaded her to eat of the forbidden fruit which would make her among the gods a goddess. Eve rejoices that it was only a dream; yet, if her waking conscience is sound, her uncensored dream had revealed the seeds of vanity and ambitious pride. Adam's psychological explanation of dreams, though in this case inadequate, brings comfort,

So all was clear'd, and to the Field they haste.

Since Satan's activity has only begun, there is irony too in the magnificent canticle in praise of God's creation which Adam and Eve utter before going to their daily work.

At this point the angel Raphael is sent down from

76

heaven to instruct Adam and reinforce the admonitions he has already received. Raphael's long narrative, which runs from book five through book eight, is of course the recapitulation of the past that we have in the *Odyssey* and the *Aeneid*, though Milton's purpose and materials are very different. Raphael commences, as we saw, with a picture of divine order, the traditional chain of being, and he emphasizes Milton's own metaphysical doctrine of the unity of matter and spirit and the perpetual transformation of matter into spirit. Then, both as a necessary part of the cosmic and epic story and as a lesson to Adam, Raphael tells of the revolt and overthrow of Satan and of the creation of the world. In the eighth book we come closer to Adam's business and bosom in the discourse on astronomy and the danger of intemperance in knowledge, of vain speculation on things remote. Adam fully agrees that the prime wisdom is the religious and moral insight needed for the problems of daily life. But as he goes on to tell the angel the story of his own experience he betrays what is to be his tragic flaw. Recalling his first union with Eve, he says:

> here passion first I felt,
> Commotion strange, in all enjoyments else
> Superior and unmov'd, here only weak
> Against the charm of Beauty's powerful glance.

He knows he should not be so carried away by an inferior being,

> yet when I approach
> Her loveliness, so absolute she seems
> And in herself complete, so well to know

Her own, that what she wills to do or say,
Seems wisest, virtuousest, discreetest, best;
All higher knowledge in her presence falls
Degraded, Wisdom in discourse with her
Loses discount'nanc't, and like folly shows;
Authority and Reason on her wait,
As one intended first, not after made
Occasionally; and to consummate all,
Greatness of mind and nobleness thir seat
Build in her loveliest, and create an awe
About her, as a guard Angelic plac't.

Those who sympathize with Satan will here sympathize with Adam and resent the frowning angel's rebuke, since for romantic naturalism the road of excess, in Blake's words, leads to the palace of wisdom—or, for another expression of the same idea:

Who liketh loving over-well
Shall look on Helen's face in Hell.
But he whose love is thin and wise
Shall see John Knox in Paradise.

Milton was not a romantic naturalist or sentimentalist, but we have seen how he glorifies love and might assume that he is here condemning it only in the way and degree in which he condemned science, or condemned Greek thought and literature in *Paradise Regained*. In all three cases he is upholding the hierarchic scale of religious and moral values against threatened violation. Adam's expression of his love for Eve is not by any means wholly bad, it is a quite human compound of right and wrong. His error is twofold. He, God's prime creature, is subordinat-

78

ing his reason (and we remember what Milton means by reason) both to his own senses and, partly because of his senses, to a being of inferior wisdom; and the implication of this double error is that he may allow his love for Eve to cloud his love for God. If we are disposed to call the author's attitude harshly Miltonic, or harshly Puritan, or anything but genuinely Christian, we may, for instance, remember some words of St. Teresa: "Cursed be that loyalty which reaches so far as to go against the law of God. It is a madness common in the world, and it makes me mad to see it. We are indebted to God for all the good that men do to us, and yet we hold it to be an act of virtue not to break a friendship of this kind, though it lead us to go against Him. Oh, blindness of the world!" [8]

Adam's answer to the angel emphasizes the chief joy of companionship and indicates that his heart is more right than his words had been, yet we are left aware of a possible weakness which temptation may bring out. Adam changes the awkward subject by asking how angels love, and his celestial visitor, after assuring him with a blush that the angelic equivalent is quite satisfactory, thinks it is time to depart. He does so with a last warning against letting passion mislead reason and will, a last reminder of Adam's responsible freedom of choice.

Adam and Eve are now left alone. The war between God and Satan had been only a macrocosmic illustration of, and background for, Milton's real theme, the war between good and evil in the soul of man; and while Satan had been defeated in heaven he is to be victorious on earth.

---

[8] *St. Teresa of Jesus*, ed. J. J. Burke (New York: Columbus Press, 1911), p. 23.

In the long invocation to the ninth book Milton repudiates
the pomp and circumstance of traditional epics for the
more truly heroic and tragic theme of human sin; and he
handles the story with much more dramatic power than
we might have expected.[9] Adam and Eve cease to be
idyllic and regal voices and turn into a very human man
and woman. Trouble begins with Eve's suggestion that
they work in different parts of the garden, a suggestion
which disturbs Adam, since they both know that evil is
lying in wait for them. Eve is full of independent pride
and reproaches her husband for his counsel against inviting a trial by herself. So "domestic" Adam—the adjective
registers Milton's opinion of his uxorious weakness—lets
her go off alone. It might be said that Eve shows more of
the spirit of *Areopagitica* than Adam, but Milton has lost
much of his old confidence in human strength. Yet his
profound pity for erring Eve is beautifully manifest in
his picture of her working alone, a picture which recalls
his earlier magical simile of the flowerlike Proserpine
about to be gathered by the prince of darkness. Here Eve
is tying up the frail stalks of flowers,

> Herself, though fairest unsupported Flow'r,
> From her best prop so far, and storm so nigh.

Even Satan is momentarily disarmed by the vision of innocent beauty. Then, in the form of a gorgeous serpent,

---

[9] See the Miltonic essays in Professor E. E. Stoll's *Poets and
Playwrights* (Minneapolis: University of Minnesota Press, 1930)
and *From Shakespeare to Joyce* (New York: Doubleday, Doran,
1944).

he makes his way to her and addresses her with seductive flattery. She is pleased by that and amazed by his gift of speech. His powers of thought and utterance, he says, are the result of eating a wondrous fruit, which he will share with her. Eve, unwary and credulous, goes with him, but when she recognizes the forbidden tree she recoils and asserts her loyalty to God and reason. Satan, pretending zeal to man, artfully gives up direct persuasion and passionately apostrophizes the tree, the source of all godlike knowledge, withheld from man by a jealous God. Eve, soliloquizing, shows that she is not consciously pursuing evil; she simply thinks that knowledge is good and therefore she should have it.[10] She is in the situation Adam had prophetically feared; her reason, surprised by a fair-appearing good, dictates false and misinforms her will. So

> her rash hand in evil hour
> Forth reaching to the Fruit, she pluck'd, she eat:
> Earth felt the wound, and Nature from her seat
> Sighing through all her Works gave signs of woe,
> That all was lost.

These last lines are not mere vague rhetoric; their import is that Eve has overthrown the natural, rational, and divine order of things. Her sin is of the same kind as Satan's, pride and presumption.

Eating greedily, she reaches what she takes to be god-

---

[10] Among many illustrations one might quote Hooker, *Of the Laws of Ecclesiastical Polity*, I, vii, 6: "For evil as evil cannot be desired: if that be desired which is evil, the cause is the goodness which is or seemeth to be joined with it." Hooker refers to Eve in the next paragraph.

like knowledge; actually it is *hybris*, infatuated irreligious self-sufficiency. Her next soliloquy, in jocund mood, shows what kind of knowledge and wisdom she has gained. She rejoices in becoming as one of the gods. Perhaps her act will remain secret; it may not have been seen by God, who is now "Our great Forbidder." God, however, is of much less concern to her than Adam. Shall she impart her knowledge to him, or rather keep it to herself,

> so to add what wants
> In Female Sex, the more to draw his Love,
> And render me more equal, and perhaps,
> A thing not undesirable, sometime
> Superior: for inferior, who is free?

Eve has acquired the same false notion of freedom that Satan had. In the end, the fear that God may punish her with death, and that Adam may then have another Eve, determines her to involve him in her own bliss or woe:

> So dear I love him, that with him all deaths
> I could endure, without him live no life.

It is a testimony to Milton's dramatic power that we believe this declaration, in spite of the very selfish quality of her love and in spite of all the calculating that has gone before and all the guile that follows. When she returns to Adam, the chief manifestation of her new knowledge, apart from her completely irreligious state of mind, is a new capacity for fibbing:

> Thee I have misst, and thought it long, depriv'd
> Thy presence, agony of love till now
> Not felt.

But she has not missed Adam, she has been having the time of her life. And after she reports the miraculous effects of the fruit, she assures Adam that she sought it chiefly for his sake. All this tale she pours forth "with Count'nance blithe," and the epithet, even more than most of the significant epithets used throughout this drama, indicates her spiritual blindness, her unawareness of the issues involved.

Adam, though chilled with horror by her avowal, is so bound to her that he resolves to share whatever punishment may come, and more than once, in the midst of his paltering with right and wrong, he appeals to the bond of nature between himself and her. Eve, happy in his loyalty, urges him to eat the fruit and enjoy new powers which make the old life seem flat and harsh. She holds out the fruit, and

> he scrupl'd not to eat
> Against his better knowledge, not deceiv'd,
> But fondly overcome with Female charm.

That is, Eve's weak reason had been deceived by an apparent good; Adam's reason tells him what is right, but his will is led astray by his love for Eve.[11] If his devotion

---

[11] Again, among many illustrations, one might quote Hooker (I, vii, 6): "Reason therefore may rightly discern the thing which is good, and yet the Will of man not incline itself thereunto, as oft as the prejudice of sensible experience doth oversway."

One might add Sir Thomas Browne's comments on Adam and Eve, from the first chapter of *Pseudodoxia Epidemica*, but I will quote the less familiar *Christian Ethics* (1675) of Thomas Traherne. The offspring of Adam and Eve, says Traherne (p. 300),

to her wins our instinctive applause, we may recall St. Teresa's words on the human loyalty that goes against the law of God, or Gerard Manley Hopkins' comments on the sinfully "chivalrous" behavior of Adam.[12] Adam is one of those people who would say, "Our country, right or wrong!" Both man and woman, well-meaning as they were, had lacked that entire and humble love of God which would have strengthened their moral judgment and moral will against two of the most universal and insidious dangers of human life, ambitious pride and sexual love.

The first result of the first sin is sensual passion, the grossest way in which human egoism violates the divine and natural order. After that second fall Adam and Eve awaken to realize something of what they have done, and to fall into bitter recrimination. Adam blames Eve and Eve can hit below the belt by asking Adam why he had not forbidden her to go off alone. Now Christ, as God's deputy, comes down to judge the guilty pair. Sin and Death emerge from hell to possess the earth. Eternal spring gives place to storms, and the golden age of peace among all creatures to jungle warfare, nature red in tooth

were destined for glory "by the Law of Nature, had not the due course of it been disturbed. Which Accident is wholy to be fathered on Adams fondness to please his Wife, and to be mothered upon her Lightness and Credulity." "Surprized by her Beauty and captivated by the Chains of Nature . . . His Appetite and Reason were united together, and both invited him to lose himself in her Embraces" (p. 298).

[12] *Further Letters of Gerard Manley Hopkins including his Correspondence with Coventry Patmore*, ed. C. C. Abbott (London: Oxford University Press, 1938), p. 194.

and claw. Adam tries to make God the cause of his sin and fate, but cannot escape the fact of his own responsibility, though he still accuses Eve. The final reconciliation between the two, a moving scene, brings them closer to each other, and to us, than they have ever been before; we hear the voices of sinful, suffering man and woman. Eve then makes a bold proposal of suicide as a means of frustrating divine punishment, but Adam rejects that as no real solution; they must humbly seek forgiveness.

If it be said that this whole drama, in Milton's handling, is far too simple to hold serious interest for a modern reader, it may also be said that here, as in Greek tragedy, we have universal motives reduced to their primary elements. Nor does Milton see his characters and their motives in mere black and white; in both Eve and Adam there is throughout a quite human mixture of good and evil. No doubt the story would be more generally read and esteemed if Adam and Eve had appealed to the right of uninhibited self-expression, or even to defective glands. We are so completely unaccustomed, in imaginative literature, to the applying of Christian standards that when Milton does so he is greeted with outcries against his stunted intelligence and imagination, his single-minded rigidity, and the like. Certainly Milton's religious and ethical imagination, like that of Aeschylus and Sophocles (not to mention the authors of the Bible), did not inhabit the never-never-land of sophisticated sentimentalism, where the difference between right and wrong is dissolved in a worship of Life, and sin is "sanctified" by "understanding."

We turn back now from drama to epic. Michael is sent

down from heaven to expel the pair from Eden, though not without the assurance that God is with man everywhere, and to unfold to Adam the future history of the race. This outline of Hebrew history may be for us rather long and dull, but some such thing was prescribed by ancient epic example and by modern treatments of the fall, and it was essential to Milton's assertion of Eternal Providence, since the story culminates with Christ's bringing the gospel of love and Christian liberty and with His sacrifice for man. Milton's total scheme is a divine comedy, a tragic fable with a happy ending, and all along he has been reminding us that greater good is to come out of evil, that Satan's triumph is not complete or final. That is his scheme and his fundamental faith, but it shines through a dark vision of human history. War and peace alike foster corruption. Religion itself becomes corrupt. And that new era which Milton had labored to bring about on earth is now relegated to the next world. Near the end of this poem of faith and hope we have such gloomy and bitter lines as these:

> Truth shall retire
> Bestuck with sland'rous darts, and works of Faith
> Rarely be found: so shall the World go on,
> To good malignant, to bad men benign,
> Under her own weight groaning, till the day
> Appear of respiration to the just,
> And vengeance to the wicked.

But that is not the poet's last word. He ends with Adam's new insight into the meaning of existence, into the nature and daily practice of the Christian life. I read the passage before and will not repeat it. If we wish to see the difference between religious humility and irreligious pride we may compare Milton's lines with the conclusion of *Prometheus Unbound*. Shelley's conception of love carries with it the worship of Man as God; and it was typical of the young revolutionary that he should make the triumph of humanitarian love in the soul of man the beginning of a new golden age of social progress and scientific dominion over nature. It was typical of the old revolutionary that the loss of an earthly paradise should leave a happier paradise to be achieved within the soul, a paradise independent of the world without and attained only through the Christian virtues for which modern man has had little use—humility, faith, and obedience.

IV

THE POETICAL TEXTURE

I HAVE EXPLAINED and, I hope, justified emphasis on Milton's poetic thought and feeling about man and God, a mode of thought and feeling which belongs to a great tradition distinctly opposed to many of the tendencies that we call modern. But to insist that Milton's vision of life is of abiding value is not to underestimate his "poetic" appeal, without which, in Renaissance terms, he might teach but could not move. And if Milton's profound earnestness of purpose was in the Renaissance tradition, so was his profound concern with poetic art. As everyone knows, Milton is recognized by friend and foe alike as the conscious and classical artist par excellence in English poetry, and *Paradise Lost* as the supreme example of the grand style. The qualities of his art, from his imaginative and emotional power to the subtleties of his rhythm and diction, have been endlessly elucidated (though the process of analysis is far from complete), and I shall not try in an hour to make a well-rounded summary of orthodox opinion. But we touched before on the opinions which anti-Miltonists have tried to set up as a new orthodoxy, and we might look a little more closely at some of them.

This hostility to Milton is, as we saw, a very conspicuous phase of the modern revolution in sophisticated taste. There is, we are told, only one real and vital kind of poetry and it is not Milton's kind. That is, to repeat the brief definition given before, poetry which simultaneously embraces diverse planes of experience and is characterized by realistic immediacy, particularity, and complexity, by a fusion of thought and feeling, by the interplay of irony and wit, and by diction, syntax, and rhythms which belong to the genius of common speech. The great exemplars, not to mention lesser ones, always display these essential qualities and Milton the rhetorician hardly ever does. To summarize the verdict of Mr. Leavis, the so-called grand style of *Paradise Lost* is in the main a heavy and monotonous stylization, a dead external grandiosity which reflects its author's narrow and rigid simple-mindedness.

While there is no very obvious link between sophisticated intellectuals and Sir Edward Marsh, I should like to quote a not irrelevant morsel from his autobiography. Sir Edward recorded that in 1931 he won a literary competition for supplying the "regrettable omission of any reference to tooth-brushing in the description of Adam and Eve retiring for the night." These are the lines he supplied:

> Yet pretermitted not the strait Command,
> Eternal, indispensable, to off-cleanse
> From their white elephantin Teeth the stains
> Left by those tastie Pulps that late they chewd
> At supper. First from a salubrious Fount
> Our general Mother, stooping, the pure Lymph

Insorb'd, which, mingl'd with tart juices prest
From pungent Herbs, on sprigs of Myrtle smeard,
(Then were not Brushes), scrub'd gumms more impearl'd
Than when young Telephus with Lydia strove
In mutual bite of Shoulder and ruddy Lip.
This done (by Adam too no less) the pair
[Straight side by side . . .[1]

I read these lines partly for their own sake but mainly because they show a cultivated reader and editor of poetry achieving, not a parody of Milton, but a parody of his worst eighteenth-century imitators, a heavy and lifeless coagulation which is far removed from Milton, though not so far from the poet seen and heard by Mr. Leavis.

As a poet whom we enjoy or do not enjoy reading, Milton must of course stand on his own feet. At the same time, as the greatest English representative of a great tradition, a central kind of poetic sensibility and technique, Milton does not stand or fall alone. He had, as our critics reluctantly admit, his own powerful individuality, yet the essential qualities of his poetic art are the same in kind as those of the ancients among whose heirs he hoped to rank. One might well apologize for asserting such a truism if it had not dropped out of sight in recent anti-Miltonic writings. It is highly significant that Mr. Eliot, who has called himself a classicist, Mr. Leavis, and the rest, do not invoke the classics; their shibboleths are always Shakespeare, Dante, and Donne, and Mr. Eliot throws in Henry James and Joyce as well. Since one cannot suspect these gentle-

---

[1] *A Number of People* (London and New York: Harper, 1939), p. 27.

men of unfamiliarity with ancient poetry, their silence can only imply a willful ignoring of what should count largely in any judgment of Milton. I do not mean that Milton deserves high marks because he imitated and echoed the classics. What I do mean, though it may seem too obvious to state, is that, since Milton's art is of the ancient kind, the charges brought against him must be brought likewise against nearly all the Greek and Roman poets. And it is doubtful if even our iconoclasts would venture to dismiss nearly all ancient poetry as bad, although that great body of writing, lyrical as well as epic, was very thoroughly stylized and artificial. Would they damn Homer and Virgil as vicious in themselves and in their influence because these poets' diction, syntax, and movement made up a very consciously "poetical" medium remote from common speech? Would they pronounce Virgilian style complicated and lifeless artifice because Virgil did not write like Plautus or Catullus or Persius? But if we agree that most ancient poets were entitled to wear their singing robes, so assuredly was their English affinity and peer.

We may again recall Mr. Leavis' general view, a view evidently shared by Mr. Eliot and others, that Milton was a man of moral force and grandeur, with a dominating sense of righteousness, a single-minded and simple-minded egoism, which made him incapable of exploring the significance and conditions of righteousness and led him to impose a merely artificial order upon experience. One might, if one's mind worked in that way, use the same words about Pindar or Aeschylus. The critics' moral judgment of Milton seems to be in part a reflection of their aesthetic judgment, and their aesthetic judgment indicates either unwillingness or incapacity to understand the methods of classical art. A poet like Donne develops his theme through a network of heterogeneous particulars and thereby displays what is called a unified sensibility, though the adjective might better be "multiple." Milton on the other hand was always governed by the traditional principle which Ben Jonson stated simply, that "the learned use ever election, and a mean; they look back to what they intended at first, and make all an even, and proportion'd body." We have a signal example of that in the beautiful lines Milton cut out of the beginning of *Comus*, apparently because they blurred his main idea; if the author of the *Anniversaries* had written such lines, or their equivalent, he would have retained and amplified them. In Milton and other truly classical artists the artistic creed, like the philosophic creed, rests on a hierarchical scale of values, not on the assumption that all the facts of experience or erudition are born free and equal. The ancient poets would have been astonished if told that their method betrayed a single-minded simplicity and ignorance of the complexities of human nature and life. They would have replied that it was the artist's job to order nature, not merely to reproduce it or leave it half-finished. I am not saying that the one method is at all times and for all purposes better than the other, I am only saying that it is foolish to confuse the self-imposed limitations of classical art with a limitation of intelligence and sensibility, and doubly foolish to write as if Milton's method were a deplorable invention of his own. When we boil down the hostile criticism of Milton's technique, much of it only amounts to the usual romantic feeling that classical art is cold and dead. There are always critics who, seeing the surface of the ocean smooth, take it for a pond, and, seeing a pond agitated by the wind, take it for the ocean. To appreciate the complexity and depth of emotional suggestion in Milton one must, so to speak, learn his language, just as one learns that a homely phrase, a lifted eyebrow, in Robert Frost or Henry James may mean more than the manifold kinds of violence in Robinson Jeffers or William Faulkner.

One pervasive element in classical art which devotees of metaphysical particularity cannot abide is its generalizing habit, its refusal to number the streaks of the tulip. In Milton, as in the ancients, that habit springs from the instinct for rendering the normal and universal, not the peculiar. The result may appear "simple," but it is not thin. One perfect example of classical writing is the invocation to Light:

> Thus with the Year
> Seasons return, but not to me returns
> Day, or the sweet approach of Ev'n or Morn,
> Or sight of vernal bloom, or Summer's Rose,
> Or flocks, or herds, or human face divine;
> But cloud instead, and ever-during dark
> Surrounds me, from the cheerful ways of men
> Cut off, and for the Book of knowledge fair
> Presented with a Universal blanc
> Of Nature's works to mee expung'd and ras'd,
> And wisdom at one entrance quite shut out.
> So much the rather thou Celestial light
> Shine inward, and the mind through all her powers
> Irradiate, there plant eyes, all mist from thence
> Purge and disperse, that I may see and tell
> Of things invisible to mortal sight.

In the first lines the generalized items—the round of seasons, "Day," so suggestively poised, "Ev'n or Morn," and the rest, including the profoundly moving surprise of the inverted "divine"—all these are packed with emotion because they are merely registered with impersonal restraint as the commonplace phenomena of every day. We feel the reserve of power behind such quietness. We are compelled to realize for ourselves what deprivation means, and we can do so because Milton universalizes his own feelings, the normal feelings of the cheerful human race to which he belongs. He feels, to be sure, as John Milton, but he writes as "the blind poet." [2] Both in temper and manner Milton's humble prayer—the prayer of a man whose imagination, according to Lord David Cecil, is "unlit by heavenly gleams"—is a world away from the passionate egoism of Donne's religious poems.

These lines, and countless others in *Paradise Lost*, are written with more or less natural and almost prosaic simplicity. But a generalized style of more ritualistic remoteness is appropriate and necessary in a long poem about God and Satan, Everyman and Everywoman, on the stage of the world. Milton's stage is completely different from Dante's and demands in general the opposite of realistic minuteness. What Milton needs to give is the idea of hell, not a road map, the idea of an earthly paradise, not a recognizable description of a spot in Mesopotamia. His generalizing habit very rarely becomes routine classicism or inflation, and the critics' expressions of dislike, when attached to actual examples and not left in a hazy grandeur

---

[2] C. S. Lewis, *A Preface to* Paradise Lost (London: Oxford University Press, 1942), p. 58.

of generality, usually reveal a failure to understand the poet's intention and achievement. We took account before of Mr. Eliot's comprehensive lack of comprehension and may look now at two passages from the picture of Eden which are condemned by Mr. Leavis. One is this:

> And all amid them stood the Tree of Life,
> High eminent, blooming Ambrosial Fruit
> Of vegetable Gold.

While the critic seems to think the Tree of Life should have been presented in terms acceptable to the horticulturist, Milton wishes, with an oblique glance at the apples of the Hesperides, to suggest a mysterious growth hardly to be approached in words. In the paradoxical phrase "vegetable Gold," which Mr. Leavis especially scorns, each word is altered and quickened by the other; the richness of "Gold" glorifies the simple product of nature, and the rich natural life implied in "vegetable" gives pliant form and vitality to metallic hardness and removes the idea of unhealthy artifice and evil which in *Paradise Lost* is associated with gold.

Mr. Leavis' other horrible example is a longer neighboring passage:

> How from that Sapphire Fount the crisped Brooks,
> Rolling on Orient Pearl and sands of Gold,
> With mazy error under pendant shades
> Ran Nectar, visiting each plant, and fed
> Flow'rs worthy of Paradise which not nice Art
> In Beds and curious Knots, but Nature boon
> Pour'd forth profuse on Hill and Dale and Plain,
> Both where the morning Sun first warmly smote

The open field, and where the unpierc't shade
Imbrown'd the noontide Bow'rs: Thus was this place,
A happy rural seat of various view:
Groves whose rich Trees wept odorous Gums and Balm,
Others whose fruit burnisht with Golden Rind
Hung amiable, Hesperian Fables true,
If true, here only, and of delicious taste.

The labored, pedantic artifice of the diction, says Mr. Leavis, suggests that Milton is focusing rather upon words than upon perceptions, sensations, or things; the conventional items "convey no doubt a vague sense of opulence, but this is not what we mean by 'sensuous richness.' " [3] In other words, Milton was trying, or should have tried, to create the sensation of being in a garden, like Marvell's perhaps, and only produced a tissue of unreal generalities. (If, by the way,

A happy rural seat of various view

is bad eighteenth-century diction, so too perhaps is Marvell's

Waves in its plumes the various light.)

While wrong-headed on the main point, Mr. Leavis has a glimmer of the truth in his vague sense of opulence. Milton knew quite as well as his critic that he was assembling the stock properties of traditional earthly paradises. Far from trying to render the sensation of being in a garden, he was suggesting, through conventional symbols, a golden age more perfect than even the classical poets had imagined. He is gathering us, in the language of Yeats, into the

---

[3] *Revaluation* (London: Chatto and Windus, 1936), p. 50.

artifice of eternity. A localized sharpness of sensation would have both cramped and dissipated that half-abstract impression of an ideal world, an ideal state both cosmic and human, external and mental. Mr. Leavis deplores the contrast between such writing and the uniquely complex and dynamic particularity of Comus' speech on the bounties of nature. But in that speech, in writing for once in a way which would win Mr. Leavis' applause, Milton was conveying the idea of vast sprawling disorder in keeping with the spiritual disorder of his naturalistic speaker.

Milton's emphasis on the fresh fertility and unspoiled simplicity of Eden is a notable instance of a general device, though "device" is hardly adequate for what is a religious and philosophic as well as an artistic principle. That is the kind of contrast which his master Spenser had first used on a large scale. In *Paradise Lost* as in *The Faerie Queene*, and to an even greater degree, there is a continuous antithesis, direct or indirect, between simplicity, purity, goodness, health, light, life, and love on the one hand, and luxury, corruption, evil, disease, darkness, death, and hate on the other. It is, however different the manner, much the same as the continuous contrast in *The Waste Land* between water and aridity as symbols of spiritual life and death. And Milton's all-embracing network of contrasts, the imaginative and pictorial illustration of right and wrong, is one of the richest elements in that power of architectural design which Mr. Leavis likens to bricklaying. When the simple-minded old poet appears to be merely letting himself go in ornamental opulence, he may be doing something more than that. Let us look first at a passage in *The Waste Land*:

The Chair she sat in, like a burnished throne,
Glowed on the marble, where the glass
Held up by standards wrought with fruited vines
From which a golden Cupidon peeped out
(Another hid his eyes behind his wing)
Doubled the flames of sevenbranched candelabra
Reflecting light upon the table as
The glitter of her jewels rose to meet it,
From satin cases poured in rich profusion;
In vials of ivory and coloured glass
Unstoppered, lurked her strange synthetic perfumes,
Unguent, powdered, or liquid—troubled, confused
And drowned the sense in odours; stirred by the air
That freshened from the window, these ascended
In fattening the prolonged candle-flames,
Flung their smoke into the laquearia,
Stirring the pattern on the coffered ceiling.[4]

Here, through a picture of physical objects (a picture perhaps somewhat overloaded for its purpose), Mr. Eliot is describing their owner's spiritual desiccation and blindness and irreligious pride. That is precisely what Milton does in describing the palace of Pandemonium built by the fallen angels in hell:

Anon out of the earth a Fabric huge
Rose like an Exhalation, with the sound
Of Dulcet Symphonies and voices sweet,
Built like a Temple, where Pilasters round
Were set, and Doric pillars overlaid
With Golden Architrave; nor did there want

---

[4] *The Waste Land*, ii (*Collected Poems*, London: Faber and Faber; New York: Harcourt, Brace, 1936).

Cornice or Frieze, with bossy Sculptures grav'n,
The Roof was fretted Gold. Not Babylon,
Nor great Alcairo such magnificence
Equall'd in all thir glories, to inshrine
Belus or Serapis thir Gods, or seat
Thir Kings, when Egypt with Assyria strove
In wealth and luxury.

Since we hear a good deal about the poverty of Milton's
rhetorical texture, we may look at a few details in this
description. The supernatural power and speed of the
diabolic builders are conveyed in the rhythm of "out of
the earth" and "Rose like an Exhalation," and in the substance of the simile. "Exhalation" was a generic name for
hot, dry "smokes" ascending from the earth, thinner and
lighter than watery "vapors"; besides, exhalations, in
themselves suggestive of diseased nature, might be kindled
into comets and other portentous apparitions. The mention of "Symphonies" recalls the miraculous building of
Ilion and Thebes, although, in contrast with the noble
music of Apollo and Amphion, the words "Dulcet" and
"sweet" suggest unhealthily sensuous Lydian airs; Milton
may have remembered too, as he had in an early sonnet,
the so-called beginning of Greek liberty, the Spartans'
destruction of the walls of Athens to the music of women
flute players. "Built like a Temple" reminds us how far this
gorgeous palace is from the simplest of true temples,

> an Island salt and bare,
The haunt of Seals and Orcs, and Sea-mews' clang,

how far from Him who prefers

> Before all Temples th' upright heart and pure.

99

"Doric pillars," which imply heroic strength, are "overlaid with Golden Architrave" and an excess of luxuriant ornament, as the builders' angelic strength has been corrupted. Finally, here as elsewhere, Milton links Satan and his host with the barbarous and mighty empires of the heathen orient, empires which are the very synonym of human pride long since overthrown, as such things must always be. Thus we visualize and feel the evil degradation of angelic powers, but at the same time the whole description and the main metrical movement reflect the angels' renewed energy and confidence. And though the general impression is quite clear, a full impression depends upon details and overtones which do not bear out the charge of Milton's insensitivity to the smaller effects of words and rhythms. His wealth of traditional and emotional association, while very different from that of Donne or Mr. Eliot, has its own complexity, a complexity, however, not tangential, as in both those poets it often is, but so coherently integrated that it seems simple.

One could not very well, in the briefest sketch of Milton, overlook his classical adaptations, although these are much less important than his classicism in the more general and deeper sense of the word. I shall not speak here of large elements in his fable, like the roll call and council of leaders, the use of celestial agencies, and so on. These things are interesting, since Milton does not imitate without re-creating, but we are concerned with the minuter threads of texture.

Of Milton's heterogeneous allusions those which spring first to mind are the mythological. Three of the four passages in Milton which Mr. Leavis is able to praise are of that kind. In Milton as in other Renaissance poets the ancient myths are generally symbols of an ideal world of ideal beauty, and the description of Eden is naturally studded with them. Mr. Eliot, in his earlier verse, was in the habit of juxtaposing a sordid present and an ideal past, and Milton, though never a romantic in the sense that Mr. Eliot was, could feel a partly similar nostalgia, sometimes in a simply idealistic mood, sometimes not. His description of the loveliest of earthly paradises was given, as we observed, after Satan had entered it, so that there was a tragically ironic contrast between ideal beauty and imminent evil. And in his pictures of Adam and Eve there is a frequent revelation, especially moving from an upholder of conscious virtue, of the desire to believe in an ideal state of unconscious innocence. Both nostalgic idealism and tragic irony are fused in the most beautiful and famous of all Milton's similes:

> Not that fair field
> Of Enna, where Proserpin gath'ring flow'rs
> Herself a fairer Flow'r by gloomy Dis
> Was gather'd, which cost Ceres all that pain
> To seek her through the world.

One cannot fully analyze the power of these lines—the poignant pattern of idea and rhythm, the pathos of familiarity in "all that pain," the implied likeness between the beauty and the fate of Proserpine and motherless Eve, and the pervasive and suggestive economy and understatement.

While there is no central antinomy in *Paradise Lost,* there may be incidental antinomies, for often, in writing a sacred poem, Milton feels obliged to label as pagan fiction what his imagination cannot resist. Perhaps the best example is the passage on Mulciber, in which he is recalling, in a serious and romantic mood and with an un-Homeric sense of space, a bit of Homeric comedy:

> how he fell
> From Heav'n, they fabl'd, thrown by angry Jove
> Sheer o'er the Crystal Battlements: from Morn
> To Noon he fell, from Noon to dewy Eve,
> A Summer's day; and with the setting Sun
> Dropt from the Zenith like a falling Star,
> On Lemnos, th' Ægæan Isle: thus they relate,
> Erring . . .[5]

The allusion is opened and closed with hostile phrases, and Mulciber is one of the fallen angels, yet the imaginative and visual richness and the rhythmical movement of the lines show the poet succumbing to the spell.

Milton's direct treatment of ancient myth is the culmination of Renaissance art and it has lost nothing of its magical beauty. But I should like to mention a few ex-

---

[5] In quoting this brief passage as a basis for comment, the acute author of *Seven Types of Ambiguity* (p. 15) rewrites it by altering two individual words and telescoping the last two lines into one:

> *flung* by angry Jove
> Sheer o'er the crystal battlements; from *dawn*
> To noon he fell, from noon to dewy eve,
> A summer's day; and with the setting sun
> Dropped into Lemnos the Ægean isle.

It is difficult to understand a sensitive critic's omitting "from the Zenith like a falling Star" or having Milton end with "Dropped into Lemnos," as if Mulciber had come to call.

amples of a device which is much more in favor with modern poets, the half-concealed or altered allusion. At the beginning of Satan's first speech he greets his lieutenant, Beelzebub, with

> If thou beest he; But O how fall'n! how chang'd
> From him, who in the happy Realms of Light . . .

We are certainly intended to remember Isaiah's "How art thou fallen from heaven, O Lucifer, son of the morning!" and almost certainly the appearance to Aeneas, at the fall of Troy, of the blood-stained ghost of Hector, "*lux Dardaniae*," "*quantum mutatus*" from that Hector who had been the tower of Trojan strength. The double allusion conveys a simultaneous effect of superhuman remoteness and grandeur and of something like concrete human reality, and also, as in Virgil, the suggestion of the end of an epoch in the world's history.

In a biblical poem classical allusions are likely to add either a romantic or a humanizing note or often, as in the simile of Proserpine, both together. The account of the creation of the universe and of men concludes with

> thrice happy if they know
> Thir happiness, and persevere upright.

Milton is clearly echoing the famous passage at the end of Virgil's second *Georgic*, in praise of the happy life of the early Italian farmers:

> O fortunatos nimium, sua si bona norint,
> agricolas!

The echo not only calls up a human and historical image of bucolic felicity but adds an overtone to the angelic warning against corrupt ambition. Another part of the same Virgilian passage appears in the invocation to Light. Even blindness, Milton declares, has not cut him off from his beloved classical authors, although they, as always, are ranked below the Bible:

> Yet not the more
> Cease I to wander where the Muses haunt
> Clear Spring, or shady Grove, or Sunny Hill,
> Smit with the love of sacred song; but chief
> Thee Sion and the flow'ry Brooks beneath
> That wash thy hallow'd feet, and warbling flow,
> Nightly I visit.

The first lines are a free paraphrase of Virgil's invocation to the learned Muses:

> Me vero primum dulces ante omnia Musae,
> quarum sacra fero ingenti percussus amore,
> accipiant . . .

"And the effect," says Mr. Tillyard,

is prodigious. Occurring, as both passages do, in contexts of a poetic intensity almost unbearable, they are like the two extremities of a flash of lightning, spots united by a blinding stream of electric fluid. In the common love of their art the two great poets as it were mingle their minds, each gaining sustenance from the other. In plainer prose, we feel Milton's context to be enriched through the reference and we trust Virgil's lines the more because they have animated the later poet.[6]

---

[6] *Poetry Direct and Oblique* (London: Chatto and Windus, 1934), p. 190. On the Homeric item (below), see *ibid.*, pp. 186–187.

We might observe how Milton turns one Homeric passage to different uses. In the fourteenth book of the *Iliad* Hera has made herself seductive for a purpose, and succeeds.

So spake he, and the son of Kronos clasped his consort in his arms. And beneath them the divine earth sent forth fresh new grass, and dewy lotus, and crocus, and hyacinth, thick and soft, that raised them aloft from the ground.

The nuptial bower of Adam and Eve is the perfection of natural beauty:

> underfoot the Violet,
> Crocus, and Hyacinth with rich inlay
> Broider'd the ground.

Incidentally, the artificial words "inlay" and "Broider'd" are employed precisely for their artificial value; the terms of sophisticated art emphasize the natural simplicity of Eden. Later Milton uses the same episode of Zeus and Hera (and a similar episode in Homer's third book, when Paris, remaining away from battle, urges Helen to dalliance). After Eve and Adam have eaten the fruit, they are both stirred by fleshly desire and Adam ends a speech of hard-boiled levity with sensual invitation:

> For never did thy Beauty since the day
> I saw thee first and wedded thee, adorn'd
> With all perfections, so inflame my sense
> With ardor to enjoy thee, fairer now
> Than ever, bounty of this virtuous Tree.

"For never once as thus," Zeus declares, "did the love of goddess or woman so mightily overflow and conquer the heart within my breast," and, after a complacent list of his conquests, he says that never before had he desired Hera herself so much. Quite apart from Homer, Adam's words, in particular the possessive animalism of "enjoy," reveal the extent of his corruption. But we may feel the irony of Adam's contrasting, in the sensual language of Zeus and Paris, his first pure and happy union with the rapture of his present carnality; even if we do not recall Homer, and if Milton did not expect us to, his own recollection was a potent factor in the result. And this is not all. Adam leads the willing Eve to a couch of flowers,

> Pansies, and Violets, and Asphodel,
> And Hyacinth, Earth's freshest softest lap.

Again we remember their first wedding, the natural beauty of their Homeric bower, and both former purity and present impurity are concentrated and contrasted in the one phrase, another ironic echo of Homer, "Earth's freshest softest lap." The whole episode, with its interplay of ideal and actual, is not less complex than, say, the coming home at the violet hour of Mr. Eliot's typist and her encounter with the small carbuncular house-agent's clerk. Indeed it might be thought more complex, since the modern episode is wholly ugly, whereas in Milton it occurs in an earthly paradise and the sensual Adam thinks he is a loving husband.

We noticed before the use of the dramatic irony of ideas in the speeches of Satan and his followers, that is, the revelation of evil attitudes which the reader is expected to assess at their true value, and that strain might be illustrated at length. Sometimes also irony is embodied, as in

Mr. Eliot, in more or less veiled allusion. Adam, when rebuked by Raphael for his excessive passion for Eve, tries to put things right and affirms that, still free, he approves the best and follows what he approves. The altered version of a familiar Ovidian tag has the effect, for the reader, of ironically puncturing Adam's self-confidence and preparing for what is to come. A more arresting instance occurs when Eve, after Adam has avowed his readiness to share her fate, exclaims,

> O glorious trial of exceeding Love!

—a phrase which at once evokes the infinite contrast between Adam's misguided love and the love of Christ for man.

It may be said that such examples of Milton's allusiveness and complexity—a few which must represent the general texture of *Paradise Lost*—only confirm the notion that he is not for every reader and everyday reading. On the other hand, for the complex sensibilities of the anti-Miltonists, he is much too simple. As a matter of logic or probability, neither position can be quite right. For many people, certainly, there does hang about Milton a forbidding austerity not only of Puritanism but of learning. It is a fact that for centuries before him, and for perhaps two centuries after him, a poet could assume in his readers, as Milton assumed, a fair amount of classical—and biblical—knowledge. If that is no longer true, we can hardly claim a large and peculiar fault in Milton or a large and peculiar merit in ourselves. But the decline of classical education, and the metaphysical revival, have brought about an odd result in a number of critical minds. Scholasticism replaced the classics as the really respectable source of images and ideas for the older poets—with this very important difference, that whereas "the classics" generally meant classical literature and thought, scholasticism has hardly ever meant scholastic philosophy but only a dialectical texture and isolated scraps of curious learning. The anti-Miltonists, however, have little interest in the ideas of Milton, they merely express abhorrence and pass on to his craftsmanship. And on that level, when Milton employs an image or idea or idiom not immediately intelligible, it is characteristic Miltonic pedantry; when Dante or Donne or Mr. Eliot does so, it is characteristic metaphysical subtlety.'

It is true of course that the more one knows of all thought and learning and literature, the richer one's understanding and enjoyment of Milton are. But the same thing may and must be said about any serious writer, the learned Donne and the unlearned Shakespeare among others. The more important fact is that Milton used to be, and still is, an essentially popular poet. For many generations a great many ordinary people read *Paradise Lost*—very often, no doubt, with a more or less unaesthetic scale of values—as ordinary people never did or could read Donne's *Anniversaries*. If those fastidious intellectuals whose noses are in great indignation at anything popular are moved to ejaculate, "So much the worse for Milton!" they must also outlaw most of the really great writings of the world, from Homer and the Bible onward. After we have listened to all that is said about Milton's remote learning and his un-English obscurity of style, we may still safely guess that about ninety per cent of his verse can be understood with sufficient ease and fullness by a modern reader of normal education and intelligence without special literary training. That reader might miss much in the way of aesthetic and philosophic refinements, though perhaps not more than sophisticated anti-Miltonists miss, and he might see a good deal more than they of what Milton strove to utter. Could that same reader comprehend ten per cent of Mr. Eliot's major poems? The question is not a peevish *argumentum ad hominem*; it has to do with the whole character and standing of poetry in Milton's age and in ours.

Then there is the complaint that *Paradise Lost* is full of dull, heavy, "unpoetic" stretches. That some parts of the poem may deserve those labels we need not deny, but they are not nearly so numerous or so long or so dull as hostile generalizations would lead one to believe. Every sympathetic reader has had the experience of finding, through his own eyes or another's, vitality and beauty in passages he had too hastily skimmed because they looked or were said to be unrewarding. Not all parts of Homer and Virgil, or even of Dante and Shakespeare and Donne, are alive for us, though anti-Miltonic references to the last three imply that these poets always thought and felt and wrote on their highest level. Dante's poetical technique does not alleviate the sour tedium of his many dull stretches, and his preoccupation with the tortures of his personal and political enemies is not more inviting to the modern reader than Milton's account of Hebrew history. Milton is surely entitled to as much allowance as other great poets of the past, and he needs no more.

If there are in *Paradise Lost* layers of material, large or small, which to us seem recalcitrant or irrelevant to the spiritual theme, we should not forget that a Renaissance epic was expected to comprehend a wide range of general learning, to embody, in a sense, the sum of knowledge. Both poets and critics believed, not without reason, that a heroic poem required a broad and solid and "prosaic" substratum. That historical reason has, to be sure, no aesthetic validity for a modern reader, but we may ask how the modern equivalent of a heroic poet meets the same problem. Milton, like all great poets before him and most poets after him, put into his text everything necessary for the understanding of the whole and the parts. Mr. Eliot, who is a very good poet, possibly a great one, achieved condensed brevity and continuously "poetic" vitality by cutting out all the expository and "prosaic" elements which the traditional epic needed. But readers of *The Waste Land* could not get very far before—and some did not get very far after—they had read his notes and gained or regained a pretty minute knowledge of Dante, Jessie Weston's *From Ritual to Romance*, Frazer's *Golden Bough*, and a multitude of casual items, like the Tarot pack of cards, from the ragbag which every individual mind contains. One may be greatly stirred by that poem without thinking that the poet's method, the often arbitrary selection of more or less private symbols, linked by an almost invisible thread of emotional and literary associations, is altogether superior to Milton's use of the central, mainly familiar, and self-sufficient traditions of mankind. Although Milton is not only richly allusive but builds on such ideas as "right reason" which are no longer familiar, while Mr. Eliot belongs to our own world, it is the contemporary poet who requires footnotes and commentary. Milton's incidental effects may be heightened by our recognition of sources, but they do not depend, as Mr. Eliot's central effects do, upon such recognition. And on the practical if not the critical plane, is the reading of Milton's occasional "prosaic" passages of verse more, or less, remote from poetic experience than the getting up of Mr. Eliot's prose authorities? It may be added, too, that in Mr. Eliot's latest work, *Four Quartets*, there is a high proportion of plain prosaic statement of a kind which the author of *The Waste Land* and many critical essays might have condemned as unpoetical.

We have not much time left to consider the charge of heavy artifice and monotony in rhythm. Those readers who have an ear for the grand style, who can hardly imagine the gap there would be in English poetry and in their own experience if *Paradise Lost* were not there, do not need any defensive comment, long or short. But, without going into technicalities, we may register a few general facts and impressions. In rhythm as in other things Milton executed *Paradise Lost* in the grand manner because nothing less than superhuman and ritualistic grandeur would be in keeping with his characters, his vast stage, and his assertion of divine order. No Renaissance poet had so critical and creative an understanding of the great principle of "decorum" as Milton. Yet within the limits of epic decorum he achieved a wide variety of tone and movement. Granted a general and necessary stylization of rhythm as of language, "the enormous onward pressure of the great stream on which you are embarked," [7] there are more or

---

[7] Lewis, *A Preface to* Paradise Lost, p. 45.

less audible differences of rhythm in Milton's descriptive, narrative, and dramatic passages. And, within those divisions, there are differences in the descriptions of hell, celestial space, and Eden, between public oratory and private dialogue and, to subdivide still further, among the several orators and between the earlier and the later dialogue of Adam and Eve. Some of the passages cited already furnish partial illustration, and out of the wealth of material we can add only two or three more. Here is the picture of Christ, the Logos, clothed with His Father's omnipotence, leaving heaven to begin the great task of creation:

> Heav'n op'n'd wide
> Her ever-during Gates, Harmonious sound
> On golden Hinges moving, to let forth
> The King of Glory in his powerful Word
> And Spirit coming to create new Worlds.
> On heav'nly ground they stood, and from the shore
> They view'd the vast immeasurable Abyss
> Outrageous as a Sea, dark, wasteful, wild,
> Up from the bottom turn'd by furious winds
> And surging waves, as Mountains to assault
> Heav'n's highth, and with the Centre mix the Pole.
> Silence, ye troubl'd waves, and thou Deep, peace.

Every rhythmic phrase reinforces the verbal picture— first the majestic order of heaven, then the vast disorder of chaos, and then, with the tremendous effect of a more drastic change of pace, the divine creation of order.

Or let us take this, from the catalogue of the fallen angels, whom old tradition transformed into the gods of the pagan religions:

> Thammuz came next behind,
> Whose annual wound in Lebanon allur'd
> The Syrian damsels to lament his fate
> In amorous ditties all a Summer's day,
> While smooth Adonis from his native Rock
> Ran purple to the Sea, suppos'd with blood
> Of Thammuz yearly wounded: the Love-tale
> Infected Sion's daughters with like heat,
> Whose wanton passions in the sacred Porch
> Ezekiel saw, when by the Vision led
> His eye survey'd the dark Idolatries
> Of alienated Judah.

Here, not through any obvious onomatopoeia but through the altered weight and tempo of rhythm, we feel the contrast between the sensuous levity of popular paganism and the passion for righteousness which inspired the Hebrew prophets.

For a specimen of dialogue we might read this early speech in which Eve is declaring her love for Adam and in which she winds and unwinds a beautiful lyrical pattern:

> With thee conversing I forget all time,
> All seasons and thir change, all please alike.
> Sweet is the breath of morn, her rising sweet,
> With charm of earliest Birds; pleasant the Sun
> When first on this delightful Land he spreads
> His orient Beams, on herb, tree, fruit, and flow'r,
> Glist'ring with dew; fragrant the fertile earth
> After soft showers; and sweet the coming on
> Of grateful Ev'ning mild, then silent Night
> With this her solemn Bird and this fair Moon,
> And these the Gems of Heav'n, her starry train:

But neither breath of Morn when she ascends
With charm of earliest Birds, nor rising Sun
On this delightful land, nor herb, fruit, flow'r,
Glist'ring with dew, nor fragrance after showers,
Nor grateful Ev'ning mild, nor silent Night
With this her solemn Bird, nor walk by Moon,
Or glittering Star-light without thee is sweet.

It would not be easy to find the equal of that in English
pastoral verse, but it is clearly not human dialogue. It is a
carefully composed poem on the beauty of human love
and its harmony with nature, and that is in keeping with
the ideal and regal order of primitive innocence. But after
Adam and Eve have sinned, their mode of utterance
changes to the natural, colloquial, and dramatic. We might
recall again that soliloquy in which we heard Eve thinking
aloud:

But to Adam in what sort
Shall I appear? shall I to him make known
As yet my change, and give him to partake
Full happiness with mee, or rather not,
But keep the odds of Knowledge in my power
Without Copartner? so to add what wants
In Female Sex, the more to draw his Love,
And render me more equal, and perhaps,
A thing not undesirable, sometime
Superior.

Or, to hear Eve in a more attractive mood of wifely con-
trition, she can speak in these faltering human accents:

Forsake me not thus, Adam, witness Heav'n
What love sincere, and reverence in my heart

I bear thee, and unweeting have offended,
Unhappily deceiv'd.

Finally, for Milton's subtlest and most inspired control
of word and rhythm, there is no greater example than the
last lines of the poem, when Adam and Eve depart from
the garden with the angel's sword flaming above the gate
behind them:

Some natural tears they dropp'd, but wip'd them soon;
The World was all before them, where to choose
Thir place of rest, and Providence thir guide:
They hand in hand with wand'ring steps and slow,
Through Eden took thir solitary way.

Every phrase and rhythm, with a marvelous depth of
suggestion, rings the changes on the mingled feelings of
sadness and hope, frailty and trust, loneliness and divine
help. In this quiet and impersonal vision of human life beginning its course on earth are concentrated all the poet's
tender pity for mankind and his unshakable faith in God
and goodness. What Milton is saying indirectly in those
simple descriptive lines is not very far from what Mr.
Eliot says directly:

Blessèd sister, holy mother, spirit of the fountain,
    spirit of the garden,
Suffer us not to mock ourselves with falsehood
Teach us to care and not to care
Teach us to sit still
Even among these rocks,
Our peace in His will
And even among these rocks

Sister, mother
And spirit of the river, spirit of the sea,
Suffer me not to be separated

And let my cry come unto Thee.[8]

It is time to take leave of Milton and I cannot do so without returning thanks to a very sympathetic audience, or rather series of audiences. But before we part I should like to emphasize again the course of Milton's spiritual evolution, his difficult attainment of profound humility. In the beginning of the Puritan revolution he had dreamed not only of helping to create God's kingdom on earth but of the glory destined for those who forwarded the great cause. In the impassioned prayer at the end of his first tract he anticipated

that day when thou, the eternal and shortly expected King, shalt open the clouds to judge the several kingdoms of the world, and distributing national honors and rewards to religious and just commonwealths, shalt put an end to all earthly tyrannies, proclaiming thy universal and mild monarchy through heaven and earth; where they undoubtedly, that by their labors, counsels, and prayers, have been earnest for the common good of religion and their country, shall receive above the inferior orders of the blessed, the regal addition of principalities, legions, and thrones into their glorious titles, and in supereminence of beatific vision, progressing the dateless and irrevoluble circle of eternity, shall clasp inseparable hands with joy and bliss, in overmeasure for ever.

---

[8] *Ash-Wednesday*, vi (*Collected Poems*, London: Faber and Faber; New York: Harcourt, Brace, 1936).

That ecstatic vision was truly religious, but Milton's religious and disinterested dreams of a better world were mixed with thoughts of glorious and regal rewards. To realize the higher and deeper and purer faith of his old age we have only to think of Abdiel and the regenerate Adam, of Christ and Samson,

> With plain Heroic magnitude of mind
> And celestial vigour arm'd.

Their trials and sufferings have purged away all thought of self or glory. Their one aim, and their one reward, is the knowledge that "in His will is our peace." And they are reflections of the true John Milton, not the arrogant egoist seen by his modern detractors. If Milton is no longer a potent influence on the modern mind, the loss is ours.

We all hope, and many believe, that the war will be followed by a return to the humanities, a return inspired, not by the notion that we can now afford useless luxuries again, but by the recognition that our modern worship of science and technology has revealed its inadequacy, and that in losing hold of the classical-Christian tradition we have lost our way. Milton is one of the greatest of the men whose experience and whose writings can help us to understand the meaning of that tradition and the true nature and goal of mankind.